Labour Law and Industrial Relations in Japan

Labour Law and Industrial Relations in Japan

by Prof. T.A. Hanami

This book was originally published as a monograph in the International Encyclopaedia for Labour Law and Industrial Relations

Second revised edition

1985

Kluwer Law and Taxation Publishers
Deventer · The Netherlands

Antwerp · Boston · Frankfurt · Londen · New York

Distribution in Canada and the USA
Kluwer Law and Taxation
190 Old Derby Street
Hingham MA 02043
USA

Library of Congress Catalog Card Number: 85-4308

ISBN 90 6544 214 6

D/1985/2664/21

Foreword

This text was prepared as a national labour law monograph for the International Encyclopaedia for Labour Law and Industrial Relations. The Encyclopaedia is a compendium of such monographs which provide concise but reasonably detailed, up-to-date information, explanation and analysis of each nation's labour law and industrial relations practice. The Encyclopaedia will provide those engaged in comparative research of industrial relations, in international business activities as well as trade union movement on an international level with comprehensive and practical knowledge.

Labour Law and Industrial Relations in Japan is being separatedly published in book form to facilitate its use to those who do not subscribe to the Encyclopaedia. Today, the Japanese industrial relations have been causing a lot of interest worldwide due to the remarkable expansion of the Japanese economy and the well-known efficiency of Japanese business. Yet, there is little material in English available on the general market concerning Japanese industrial relations. Especially, there hardly exists a book which systematically describes the Japanese industrial relations system and, in particular, the labour law system. Most of the books and articles in English on Japanese industrial relations are written by Western specialists and quite often focuss only on certain specific fields depending on the author's interests. Furthermore, the author of this monograph is not only an academic in the field of labour law and industrial relations but also a practitioner engaged in the actual dispute settlement and in the adjudication procedure as a public commissioner of Tokyo Metropolitan Labour Relations Commission. In this capacity, the author has a lot of experience in handling cases of multinational enterprises operating in Japan. The author has also participated in a number of international Conferences, comparative studies, joint projects with Western academics and field research in the advanced as well as in the developing countries. He has also experience in teaching and research activities at several Western Universities.

After 1979, when the first edition of this book was published, some significant changes took place in Japanese industrial relations, particularly caused by strains in the Japanese economy resulted from the oil crisis and the international reactions against the tremendous expansion of Japanese business activities abroad. In this second edition some extensive revisions and additional writing have been carried out to cover this new trend. The statistics and other data have also been updated.

The author has put much effort in providing the best opportunity to understand the rather unique systems and practices of Japanese industrial relations in Western and, perhaps, universal terminology and points of view. Thus, the author sincerely hopes that this book will promote the international mutual understanding of the industrial relations systems of very diverse societies in the World. Of course, it was a rather difficult task to adequately explain and analyse the Japanese culture and social context within the limit of the universal requirements of the Encyclopaedia.

For those who wish to obtain more advanced knowledge of the cultural and sociological background of the Japanese industrial relations, the author's book, in English, entitled *Labor Relations in Japan Today* (Tokyo: Kodansha International, 1979), and T. Shirai (ed.), *Contemporary Industrial Relations in Japan* (Wisconsin: University of Winconsin Press, 1984) will be helpful.

Table of Contents

List of Abbreviations 11

Introduction 13

I. The General Background 13

§1. Geography and Climate 13
§2. Political Development after 1868 13
§3. Economic Development in Modern Japan 15
§4. Economic Development after the War 16
§5. Population and Labour Force 17
§6. Income Level and Income Distribution 24
§7. Social and Cultural Values 27

II. Definitions and Notions 30

§1. Social Security Law 30
§2. Labour Law 32
I. Individual Labour Law 33
II. Collective Labour Law 34
III. Legal Nature 34
§3. Categories of Employees 36
§4. Leading Personnel – Supervisors 37

III. Historical Background 39

§1. The Pre-War Period 39
§2. Post-War Industrial Relations 41
I. The Formation of Enterprise Unionism 41
II. The Function of Enterprise Unions 41
III. Industrial Unions and National Centres 42
IV. Recent Changes and Developments 43

IV. The Role of the Government 47

§1. The Autonomy of the Social Partners 47
§2. Government Institutions 47

I. The Ministry of Labour 47
II. Labour Inspection 48
III. The Labour Relations Commissions 48

V. Sources of Labour Law 49

§1. The Constitution 49
§2. Legislation 49
§3. Collective Agreements and Rules of Work 50
§4. Cases and Legal Theories 51
§5. Custom and Practice 51
§6. International Sources 52

VI. Selected Bibliography 53

§1. Industrial Relations and Social Background 53
§2. Law in General 53
§3. Labour Law 54
I. Legislation 54
II. Articles 54
III. Periodicals 54

Part I. The Individual Employment Relationship 55

Chapter I. Definitions and Concepts 55

§1. The Different Categories of Employees 55
§2. The Different Sorts of Individual Labour Contracts 55
I. The Individual Contract for an Indefinite Period 56
II. The Individual Contract for a Definite Period 56
§3. The Probation (Trial) Period 57
§4. Regulations concerning the Conclusion of Individual Contracts 58
§5. Contractual Capacity and Restrictions on Employment 59
I. Minors 59
II. Women 59
III. Foreign Workers 60

Chapter II. Rights and Duties of the Parties in the Course of the Employment Relationship 60

§1. Employees' Duties 61
I. The Duty to Work 61
II. The Duty to Respect Professional Secrets 63
§2. Employers' Duties 64
I. The Duty to Provide Work 64
II. The Provision of Decent Working Conditions 65

III. The Establishment of Work Rules, etc. 65
IV. The Employer's Obligations at the End of the Labour Contract 66

CHAPTER III. HOURS OF WORK, OVERTIME AND HOLIDAYS 67

§1. Hours of work 67
§2. Holidays 68
§3. Overtime 69
§4. Night work 69
§5. Annual Vacations 69

CHAPTER IV. THE PROTECTION OF WOMEN AND MINORS 71

§1. The Protection of Women Workers in General 71
§2. Maternity Protection 71
§3. Discrimination and Equality 71
§4. The Protection of Minors 73

CHAPTER V. REMUNERATION AND BENEFITS 74

§1. Pay Systems 74
§2. The Notion of Wages 77
§3. Regulations concerning the Payment of Wages 78
§4. Guarantee of the Payment of Wages on the Employer's Insolvency 79
§5. The Minimum Wage 79
§6. Wage Levels 80
§7. Equal Pay 80
§8. Remuneration during Time-Off 82
I. Rest-Day Allowances 82
II. Accidents at Work and Occupational Diseases 82
III. Leave of Absence 83
§9. The Suspension Period 83

CHAPTER VI. THE TERMINATION OF THE INDIVIDUAL LABOUR CONTRACT 85

§1. Job Security in General 85
§2. Ending the Contract other than by Dismissal 86
§3. Termination by the Employee or by Agreement 86
§4. Dismissal with Notice 87
§5. Dismissal without Notice 87
§6. Reasons for Dismissal – 'Just Cause', Abusive Dismissal 88
I. Individual Dismissal 88
II. Collective Dismissal 89
§7. Redundancy 90
I. Employment Stabilisation Fund System 90

II. Measures for Employment Opportunity Creation 91
III. Specific Employment Measures 92
§8. Disciplinary Discharge 93
§9. Early Retirement System 94
§10. Termination of Special Kinds of Employment Contracts 96
§11. Regulations regarding the End of the Contract 97

CHAPTER VII. COVENANTS OF NON-COMPETITION, INVENTIONS BY EMPLOYEES 98

§1. Covenants of Non-Competition 98
§2. Inventions by Employees 99

Part II. Collective Labour Relations 101

CHAPTER I. THE RIGHT TO ORGANISE 102

§1. *Bona Fide* Trade Unions and Qualified Unions 102
§2. Freedom of Association and the Right to Organise 103
§3. The Right to Organise and Union Security 104
§4. The Right to Organise and Individual Workers 104
§5. The Right to Organise and Relations with the Unions 105
§6. Trade Union Property 105
§7. Internal Union Affairs and Members' Rights 106
§8. Trade Union Freedom in Japan and the ILO Conventions 107

CHAPTER II. THE TRADE UNIONS AND EMPLOYERS' ASSOCIATIONS 108

§1. The Trade Unions 108
§2. The Employers' Associations 112

CHAPTER III. INSTITUTIONALISED RELATIONS BETWEEN EMPLOYERS AND TRADE UNIONS 114

§1. The Enterprise Level 114
§2. The Local Level 116
§3. The Industrial Level 116
§4. The National Level 117

CHAPTER IV. COLLECTIVE BARGAINING 119

§1. The Significance of Collective Bargaining 119
§2. The Parties to Collective Bargaining 119
§3. Bargaining Sessions 120
§4. The Issues for Collective Bargaining 121
§5. Collective Bargaining and Workers Consultation 121

§6. Bargaining in Good Faith 122
§7. The Conclusion of Collective Agreements 123
§8. The Term of the Collective Agreement and its Termination 123
§9. Legal Effect of the Collective Agreement 124
I. The Contents of the Collective Agreement 124
II. Normative Effect 124
III. Obligatory Effect 126
IV. The So-Called 'Institutional' Effect 127
V. The Peace Obligation 127
VI. Extension of the Effect of a Collective Agreement 128
VII. The Effect of a Collective Agreement after its Termination 129

CHAPTER V. ACTS OF DISPUTE 131

§1. The Notion of Acts of Dispute 131
§2. Proper Acts of Dispute 131
I. Acts of *Bona Fide* Unions 131
II. The Purpose of the Act of Dispute 132
III. Proper Acts of Dispute 132
§3. Different Types of Acts of Dispute 133
I. Strikes 133
II. Going-Slow (Soldiering), Working-To-Rule etc. 136
III. Taking Holidays 136
IV. Pasting Posters, Wearing Ribbons etc. 137
V. Picketing and Sit-Downs 138
VI. Control of the Means of Production or of Management itself 138
§4. Legal Effect of the Act of Dispute 139
I. Civil Indemnity 139
II. Criminal Indemnity 140
III. Legel Effect of an Act of Dispute on the Union Movement 140
IV. Acts of Dispute and Wages 141
V. Lock-Outs 142
§5. Restriction and Prohibition of Acts of Dispute 143
I. Prohibition of Acts of Dispute which Endanger Human Life 143
II. Restriction of Acts of Dispute in Public Welfare Work 143
III. Emergency Adjustment and Acts of Dispute 143
IV. Prohibition of Acts of Dispute in the Public Sector 144

CHAPTER VI. THE LAW ON UNFAIR LABOUR PRACTICES 146

§1. The Unfair Labour Practices System 146
§2. What amounts to an Unfair Labour Practice? 146
I. Discrimination 146
II. Refusal to Bargain 149
III. Control of, or Interference in Union Administration 150
§3. The Parties to Unfair Labour Practices 150

I. Unions and Individual Workers 150
II. The Employer 151
§4. Commissioners' Orders 151

CHAPTER VII. DISPUTE SETTLEMENT 152

§1. Different Categories of Industrial Conflicts and their Settlement 152
I. Categories of Industrial Disputes 152
II. Different Disputes and their Settlement 152
§2. The Labour Relations Commissions 154
I. The Organisation of the Labour Relations Commissions 154
II. The Functions of the Commissions 155
A. Adjudication procedures in unfair labour practice cases 155
B. Dispute settlement by conciliation, mediation and arbitration 157
C. Dispute settlement in public welfare work 158
§3. Dispute Settlement in the Public Sector 159
§4. The Overlapping Jurisdictions of the Labour Relations Commissions and the Courts 159

Table of Statutes 163

Index 165

List of Abbreviations

Chūritsurōren	: Federation of Independent Unions
CLRC	: Central Labour Relations Commission
Dōmei	: Japanese Confederation of Labour
IMF-JC	: Japanese Council of Metal Workers' Union-International Metal Workers' Federation
Keidanren	: Japanese Industrialist Association
LLRC	: Local Labour Relations Commission
LPELR Law	: Local Public Enterprise Labour Relations Law
PCNELR Commission	: Public Corporation and National Enterprise Labour Relations Commission
PCNELR Law	: Public Corporation and National Enterprise Labour Relations Law
Shinsanbetsu	: National Federation of Organisations
Sōhyō	: General Council of Trade Unions of Japan
Zenmin Rōkyō	: Japanese Private Sector Trade Union Council.

Introduction

I. The General Background

§1. Geography and Climate

1. Japan consists of four main islands and thousands of smaller islands and islets lying off the eastern coast of the Asian continent in an arc 3,800 kilometres (2,360 miles) long. It covers an area of 377,435 square kilometres (145,730 square miles). Japan's total land area is about one-twenty-fifth that of the United States, one-ninth that of India, and one-and-a-half times as big as that of the United Kingdom. In terms of world land area, Japan occupies less than 0.3 per cent.

2. The climate is generally mild, although it varies considerably from place to place and the four seasons are clearly distinct. The combination of plentiful rainfall and a temperate climate produces rich forests and luxurious vegetation. But these climatic advantages are offset by the fierce topography. While Japan has a long and rocky coastline with many small but excellent harbours, mountains cover about 72 per cent of the total land area.

3. Being an archipelago, Japan has been fairly independent of foreign influence in terms of politics and culture. The comparatively mild climate also means that Japan is able to be self-sufficient in food production, although poor natural resources supporting a massive population have forced the people to live the simple and hard-working lives which today constitute a moral feature of the Japanese people.

§2. Political Development after 1868

4. The modernisation of Japan started in 1868, the year of the Meiji Restoration. The Constitution of the Empire of Great Japan established a kind of constitutional monarchy, and provided for a Diet of elected representatives, a bill of rights (though under the 'reservation of the law') and an independent judiciary. Compared with the political regime prior to the Restoration, it was definitely a step forward in the direction of modernisation. But the Constitution itself was certainly conservative, mainly because of the imperial retention of comprehensive prerogative powers. The draftsmen of the Constitution envisaged a strong bureaucracy consisting of civil and military branches, with prestige and honours emanating from the semi-divine emperor. The Diet was not to be allowed any direct control over the executive power, and even in matters of legislation and finance its authority was to be limited by the imperial prerogatives. Thus, the development of party politics in a democratic sense was hardly to be expected in pre-war Japan and was destined to be suffocated under military rule after the 1930's.

5. Under the Constitution of 1946, drafted during the Allied occupation with a view to the democratisation of Japan, the emperorship was retained but only as 'the symbol of the State and the unity of the people' (Const. Art. I). The executive supremacy contemplated by the old Constitution was replaced by legislative supremacy. The consitutional position of the judiciary was elevated by including administrative matters in its jurisdiction which were outside it under the Meiji Constitution. Human rights, with some additions, are enumerated and are to be guaranteed by the judiciary. As befits the constitution of a twentieth-century industrial state, the Constitution imposes not only the negative duty to refrain from violating human rights and fundamental freedoms but also the positive duty to promote the economic and social welfare of its citizens. That is, it provides not only such classical liberties as freedom of thought, conscience, religion, assembly and association, as well as equality under the law; but also such rights as the right to maintain a wholesome and cultured standard of living, the right to work and the workers' right to organise, to bargain collectively and to strike.

6. Under the new Constitution the Japanese people enjoy complete freedom to organise and participate in political parties and other political organisations including pressure groups and trade unions. However, political development in post-war Japan is characterised by one distinguishing feature: the continuous rule of the conservative parties, except for one short period of Socialist government during 1947–1948. Among several complex reasons for this dominance of the conservatives in post-war Japanese politics, only a few major points which are relevant to the understanding of the trade union movement and labour relations in present-day Japan will be mentioned here.

7. The powerful position of the conservative parties, including the Liberal Democratic Party which is the present ruling party, is to be explained by strong support received from the business group and a close bond with the bureaucracy. This strength is, at the same time, a reflection of the weakness of the progressive parties. Because of the differences between the reform parties and the revolutionary parties they have had very little chance of gaining power and have never been ready to establish positive plans and programmes; devoting their energy instead to criticising the government and the ruling party and to fighting each other. Table I shows the political composition of the Diet after the 1984 election. The ruling Liberal Democratic Party holds a bare majority together with the New Liberal Club, although all the other parties advocating some type of reform will hardly compete against the Liberal Democrats as a single party. However after the election of 1984 when the Liberal Democrats declined seriously and the two moderate parties, the Komei and the Democratic Socialists, increased their seats, the prospects of a coalition government, including reformists, emerged.

TABLE I

Political Party Composition of the Diet as of January 1984

	House of Representatives	House of Councillors
Liberal Democratic Party	250	136
Japanese Socialist Party	112	43
Komei Party	58	27
Democratic Socialist Party	38	13
Japanese Communist Party	26	14
New Liberal Club	8	–
Others	19	16
Vacancies	–	3
Total	511	252

Source: Ministry of Home Affairs.

§3. ECONOMIC DEVELOPMENT IN MODERN JAPAN

8. Considering such serious disadvantages as its small size, poor natural resources, massive population, late coming of modernisation and the destruction of the economy during the Second World War, it is often called a miracle that Japan is now ranked third in the world in terms of economic scale. This rapid industrialisation within 100 years and complete economic rehabilitation after the War stem from numerous factors, a few of which will be mentioned here very briefly.

9. Industrialisation started much later than in Western countries, and the fact that it proceeded so remarkably fast may be attributed to the strong initiative taken by the Government. During the feudal age Japan had managed to acquire a well-educated population, well-developed administrative organs and an accumulation of energy in a society which had been secluded for 300 years. The Government was able to release this ripe energy and stimulate enthusiasm among the people for Western civilisation by introducing new legal and social institutions, modern technology and a modern educational system. As one of these modernisation measures the Government ventured to invest in and initiate most of the key industries, such as cotton spinning, silk reeling, iron and steel, ship-building, machinery, railways, shipping and so on.

10. The Japanese virtue of working hard and being content with a simple life can be regarded as the Japanese version of the 'Protestant work ethic' of Max Weber. However, although a modest amount of commercial capital had been accumulated in the hands of wealthy merchants in the feudal era, the capital accumulation was hardly enough for industrial development. The Government transferred some of the undertakings it had established to the leading merchants under favourable conditions, and encouraged their development by providing privileges and aid in terms of finance and legal and institutional help. Very close ties were created in this way between the Government and industry, which remain very important today in understanding the Japanese economy and Japanese society.

11. The Meiji Government did not transfer all its undertakings to private business, but instead kept some of the most important industries, such as munitions factories and related industries, to run itself. Such Government industries have been playing a major role in providing highly skilled labour and management techniques for Japanese capitalism.

§4. Economic Development after the War

12. At the end of World War II, Japan lost all of its overseas territories. Production facilities had also suffered heavy damage. About one-third of the national wealth accumulated as a result of industrialisation since the Meiji Restoration was lost. The combination of the Japanese people's efforts towards recovery and a relatively favourable international setting, including American assistance, enabled the Japanese economy to reach its pre-war level in less than 10 years. After that, the economy continued to grow with a surprisingly rapid average annual growth rate of 9.0 per cent in the 1950's and 11.2 per cent in the 1960's. That is, the Japanese economy expanded two or three times as fast as the economies of other major industrial nations. The 1974 GNP stood at $451,700 million. Although this is less than one-third of the American GNP of $1,397,400 million for the same year, it ranks second in the free world.

13. Among the various industries, the recovery of mining and manufacturing was the most remarkable. In 1946, right after the War, production in these industries had dropped to 27.6 per cent of its pre-war level (1934–1936); but after it reached its pre-war level in 1951 it rose steadily, and recorded 3.5 times that in 1960. During the sixties it continued to rise almost fourfold. Japan is now first in the world in the production of ships, radios and television sets, second in automobiles and rubber products, and third in cement and iron and steel.

14. During this period of rapid growth, especially in the later years, Japan's external trade developed quite remarkably. Exports have risen at an average annual rate of 12.3 per cent during the 10 years between 1964 and 1974. In 1974, Japan's exports totalled $55,536 million and its share in aggregate free world exports was 7.2 per cent. In 1981, exports reached $152,030, sharing 8.5 per cent of total free world exports. At the same time, imports have increased four-fold, from $8,165 million in 1965 to $62,100 million in 1974, representing 8.1 per cent of total world imports for that year. In 1981, the imports totalled $143,290 and represented 7.8 per cent of free world imports. Parallel to the growth of trade has been a change of pattern, shifting from light industry to the heavy and chemical industries. While in the 1950's light industry products still accounted for about half of Japan's export value, in 1974 heavy and chemical industry products accounted for about 82 per cent.

15. Thus, Japan's industrial development in recent decades has been characterised by a steady drop in the importance of labour-intensive industries such as textiles and sundries, while capital-intensive industries such as chemicals, steel and machinery have grown considerably. However, because of the energy crisis and emerging environmental problems in these few years, such a pattern of growth is now facing great difficulties. Another problem with regard to the future development of the Japanese economy is the problem of social welfare. While the rapid growth of the past quarter century has given Japan the second highest ranking GNP in the free world, the per capita national income stood at $7,421 in 1979, placing Japan 17th or 18th in the free world and lower than most of the industralised nations in Europe and North America. Also, such problems as poor housing, roads and other environmental facilities, the delay or neglect of modernising agriculture and small- and medium-sized enterprises, the destruction of nature (including pollution) and increasing social tension have been emerging in recent years and will present a serious challenge to future development.

§5. Population and Labour Force

16. Japan's labour force in 1982 numbered 52,774,000, of which 2.4 per cent was totally unemployed. The industrial distribution of the employed in 1980 was as follows:

Table II

The Gainfully Employed by Industry in 1980 (in thousands)

All industry	55,811
Agriculture and Forestry	5,649
Fishery and Aquaculture	461
Mining	108
Construction	5,383
Manufacturing	13,246
Wholesale and Retail	12,731
Finance, Insurance and Real Estate	2,004
Transportation, Communication and other Public Utilities	3,853
Services	10,288
Public Service	2,026

Source: Ministry of Labour, White Paper on Labour, 1983.

17. The distribution of the labour force has changed completely in accordance with the change in the industrial structure in the post-war period. The percentage of the labour force employed in primary industry declined from 41 per cent in 1955, to 24.7 per cent in 1965, to 19.3 per cent in 1970 and then to less than 10 per cent in 1980. In contrast, the portion of the labour force employed in secondary and tertiary industry increased (see Table III). Within

Table III

The Change in the Industrial Distribution of the Employed

	1930	1940	1945	1950	1960	1965	1970	1975	1980
Total (A)	2,934	3,223	3,563	3,926	4,369	4,763	5,204	5,314	5,581
Primary Industry	1,449	1,419	1,721	1,611	1,424	1,175	1,007	735	611
Secondary Industry	599	842	781	922	1,276	1,522	1,765	1,809	1,873
(Manufacturing)	(470)	(685)	(569)	(690)	(955)	(1,151)	(1,344)	(1,323)	(1,324)
Tertiary Industry	879	940	1,057	1,393	1,668	2,066	2,431	2,752	3,090
B/A (%)	49.6	44.1	48.3	41.0	32.9	24.7	19.3	3.8	10.9
C/A (%)	20.5	26.4	22.0	23.5	29.1	31.9	33.9	34.0	33.5

Note: B = Primary Industry; C = Secondary Industry.
The real numbers of this Table are in ten thousand counting fractions of 5 and over as units and cutting away the rest.
Source: Bureau of Statistics, Office of the Prime Minister, National Population Census.

secondary industry the increase in those employed in manufacturing industries has been remarkable, and within this category the portion of those employed in heavy and chemical industries has increased while the portion employed in light industries has declined. The percentage of the labour force employed in metal, machinery and related industries, as against all manufacturing industries, increased from 33.6 per cent in 1956 to 44.8 per cent in 1965. However, the proportion of secondary industry as a whole stopped increasing after 1970 while that of tertiary industry increased steadily from 38.2 per cent in 1960 to 46.6 per cent in 1970 and to 55.4 per cent in 1980.

18. In accordance with the change in industrial distribution described above, the structure of the employment status of the labour force has also changed drastically. The percentage of wage earners among the gainfully employed increased from about 40 per cent in 1955 to 65 per cent in 1970, 68 per cent in 1975 and 71.7 per cent in 1980. During the 20 years from 1955 to 1975 the ratio of employees as against self-employed and unpaid family workers has reversed almost completely from 4 : 6 to 7 : 3. (see Table IV). The numbers in the labour force and the labour force participation rates by age group and sex are to be found in Tables V and VI. With regard to these figures, two points are worth noting. First, the marked decline in labour participation rates among the young, especially those between 15 and 19 years of age (Table V). This is mainly due to the trend towards higher education in the younger generation, and the recent decline in the birth rate will accentuate the shortage of young workers in the future. During the labour shortage experienced in Japan since the mid-sixties the demand for younger labour has been extremely high, while that for middle-aged or older workers has been quite low. As a result of another recent trend, that towards higher life expectancy, this trend will continue to cause problems in the Japanese labour market of the future. Secondly, the decline in the aggregate labour force participation ratio during the period from the mid-fifties to 1975 has been largely due to the conspicuous reduction in the aggregate female participation ratio (Table VI). But this decline reflects not so much a change in the labour supply behaviour of females, *per se*, as a major decline in the importance of agriculture. On the contrary, as far as employees are concerned, the size of the female labour force has increased significantly. The number of female employees which was 5.3 million in 1955 reached over 11 million in 1975, and over 14 million in 1982, almost tripling in number. The growth in the number of female employees has been caused mainly by the labour shortage during the late 1960's and the early 1970's. As a result of the increased demand for other possible sources of labour arising from the shortage of junior and senior high school graduates, housewives who had not been working started to work and younger female workers who had been leaving work after marriage began to stay in employment. Thus, the percentage of women over 30 years of age out of the total number of female employees went up from 36 per cent in 1960 to 66.7 per cent in 1982. The percentage of married women out of the total number of female employees also went up, from 34.8 per cent in 1955 to 78.5 per cent in 1982.

TABLE IV

Employment Status of the Gainfully Employed: 1940–1980

	All industries				
Sex and year	Total	Self-employed (A)	Unpaid family workers (B)	Employees (C)	Percentage of employees in the labour force C / A + B + C
Total					
1940	3,223	845	1,026	1,350	41.9
1948	3,332	821	1,297	1,213	36.4
1950	3,557	929	1,224	1,396	39.3
1955	3,926	939	1,224	1,396	45.8
1960	4,369	968	1,050	2,349	53.8
1965	4,761	934	928	2,891	60.7
1970	5,223	1,015	853	3,354	64.2
1975	5,223	939	628	3,646	69.8
1980	5,536	951	603	3,971	71.7
Males					
1940	1,959	720	274	964	49.2
1948	2,062	709	434	918	44.5
1950	2,181	760	381	1,035	47.5
1955	2,389	759	342	1,286	53.9
1960	2,660	738	284	1,638	61.6
1965	2,903	709	211	1,978	68.1
1970	3,176	730	180	2,265	71.3
1975	3,270	658	127	2,479	75.8
1980	3,394	658	112	2,617	77.1
Females					
1940	1,263	124	752	386	30.6
1948	1,270	112	862	295	23.2
1950	1,376	169	843	361	26.2
1955	1,536	180	846	510	33.2
1960	1,708	230	766	710	41.6
1965	1,857	224	716	913	49.2
1970	2,046	284	673	1,088	53.2
1975	1,953	280	501	1,167	59.1
1980	2,142	293	491	1,354	63.2

Source: Bureau of Statistics, Office of the Prime Minister, Annual Report on the Labour Force Survey.

(in 10,000s)

Agriculture (including forestry but excluding fishing)				Non-agricultural industries			
Self-employed	Unpaid family workers	Employees	Percentage of employees in the labour force	Self-employed	Unpaid family workers	Employees	Percentage of employees in the labour force
467	846	49	3.6	375	179	1,280	69.7
511	1,134	64	3.7	306	158	1,113	70.5
544	1,037	71	4.3	383	187	1,324	69.8
512	961	66	4.3	426	227	1,730	72.6
504	811	51	3.8	464	239	2,297	76.5
445	628	36	3.3	487	299	2,853	78.4
406	519	28	3.0	608	334	3,323	77.9
303	286	29	4.6	636	342	3,617	78.7
253	249	30	5.6	698	354	3,941	78.9
408	209	34	5.3	312	354	3,941	70.9
442	355	45	5.3	263	77	847	71.3
458	309	48	5.9	301	72	986	72.6
437	264	47	6.3	322	78	1,239	75.6
401	203	33	5.3	336	80	1,604	79.4
362	133	25	4.9	346	78	1,951	82.1
313	97	20	4.6	416	82	2,244	81.8
223	51	21	7.1	435	76	2,459	82.7
196	43	21	8.0	462	69	2,596	83.0
60	636	155	2.2	63	115	364	67.0
69	778	192	2.2	42	81	266	68.3
86	728	225	2.7	82	115	338	63.1
75	697	194	2.4	104	148	491	68.7
103	607	177	2.4	127	158	693	70.7
82	495	113	1.9	141	221	901	71.3
92	421	84	1.6	191	251	1,079	70.9
79	235	8	2.4	201	266	1,159	71.3
57	206	9	3.3	236	285	1,345	72.0

TABLE V

Population, Labour Force and Labour Force Participation Rates by Age Group: 1955, 1965, 1970 and 1982 (in 10,000s)

Year and age group	Total population			Labour force			Labour Force participation rate (%)		
	Total	Males	Females	Total	Males	Females	Total	Males	Females
1955									
Total aged 15 and older	5,947	2,868	3,079	3,990	2,438	1,552	67.1	85.0	50.4
Aged 15–19	862	434	428	445	223	212	51.7	53.7	49.6
Aged 20–24	840	419	420	651	366	284	77.5	87.4	67.6
Aged 25–29	760	377	382	560	362	198	73.7	95.9	51.8
Aged 30–39	1.123	511	611	814	499	315	72.5	97.5	51.6
Aged 40–49	931	446	485	798	432	266	85.8	97.1	54.8
Aged 50–59	705	353	351	501	330	171	71.0	93.3	48.6
Aged 60 and older	724	325	398	318	214	104	44.0	65.9	26.2
1965									
Total aged 15 and older	7,310	3,542	3,767	4,829	2,951	1,877	66.1	83.3	49.8
Aged 15–19	1,085	547	537	413	211	201	38.1	38.7	37.5
Aged 20–24	906	449	457	710	393	317	78.4	87.5	69.5
Aged 25–29	836	415	420	603	407	196	72.1	98.0	46.6
Aged 30–39	1,575	789	786	1,186	773	413	75.3	98.0	52.6
Aged 40–49	1,088	495	592	853	483	369	78.4	97.6	62.4
Aged 50–59	866	410	455	645	395	249	74.5	96.3	54.8
Aged 60 and older	952	434	518	416	287	129	43.7	66.1	25.1
1970									
Total aged 15 and older	7,889	3,822	4,066	5,294	3,224	2,070	67.1	84.3	50.9
Aged 15–19	906	457	449	327	166	161	36.2	36.5	35.8
Aged 20–24	1,066	531	534	822	443	378	77.2	83.5	70.9
Aged 25–29	908	451	457	649	443	206	71.5	98.2	45.1
Aged 30–39	1,657	830	827	1,246	818	428	75.2	98.5	51.7
Aged 40–49	1,321	634	687	1,064	623	440	80.5	98.2	64.1
Aged 50–59	923	419	503	691	402	289	75.0	95.8	57.5
Aged 60 and older	1,105	497	607	492	326	166	44.5	65.5	27.3
1982									
Total aged 15 and older	9,116	4,430	4,687	5,774	3,522	2,252	63.3	79.5	48.0
Aged 15–19	833	426	407	147	77	70	17.6	18.0	17.1
Aged 20–24	787	399	387	555	240	275	70.5	60.1	71.0
Aged 25–29	829	417	412	611	402	210	73.7	96.4	50.9
Aged 30–39	2,002	1,005	998	1,521	982	540	75.9	97.7	54.1
Aged 40–49	1,698	846	851	1,383	824	557	81.4	97.3	65.4
Aged 50–59	1,372	664	709	1,013	622	391	73.8	93.6	55.1
Aged 60 and older	1,596	672	923	543	335	208	34.0	49.8	22.5

Source: Bureau of Statistics, Office of the Prime Minister, Annual Report on the Labour Force Survey.

TABLE VI

Labour Force Participation Ratio

(units: percentages)

Year	Total	Male	Female
1955	70.8	85.9	54.6
1960	69.2	84.8	54.5
1965	65.7	81.7	50.6
1970	65.4	81.8	49.9
1971	65.4	82.2	48.8
1972	64.4	82.1	47.7
1973	64.7	82.2	48.3
1974	63.7	81.8	46.5
1975	63.0	81.4	45.7
1976	63.0	81.2	45.8
1977	63.2	80.6	46.6
1978	63.4	80.3	47.4
1979	63.4	80.2	47.6
1980	63.3	79.8	47.6
1981	63.3	79.8	47.7
1982	63.3	79.5	43.0

Source: Office of the Prime Minister, Bureau of Statistics, Labour Force Survey.

19. In 1982, the total number of employees in all industries was 41 million, of which 35.8 were employed by private industry. The remaining 5.2 million, were employed in the public sector and can be divided into the following four categories: national government employees, 840,000; local government employees, 2.96 million; employees in public corporations and national government enterprises, 1.15 million; employees in local government enterprises, 250,000.

20. The Japanese have been integrated into a monolithic nation and have lived a monocultural life for more than 15 centuries without any significant racial mixture. Thus there exist very few minority problems in Japanese society, especially in employment relations. In the pre-war period there were a fairly significant number of foreign workers, mostly Koreans and Chinese, and they were sometimes discriminated against as distinct minority groups both in employment and in society in general. But since the war the Government has adopted a very strict policy to prevent an influx of foreign workers onto the Japanese labour market; and so now any problems of discrimination in employment are mostly encountered by women and trade union activists.

§6. Income Level and Income Distribution

21. Table VII shows how families were distributed according to their income in 1980. The lowest quarter of families earned less than 2.10 million yen, the lower half earned less than 3.22 million yen and the lowest three-quarters, less than 4.70 million yen (see Figure I). Since the average income of each family was about 3.7 million yen, about 60 per cent of all families earned less than the average in 1980. However, income distribution in Japan has shown a trend towards equalisation in recent years. Figure II illustrates this trend between 1963 and 1970 in a Lorenz curve.

Table VII

Family Distribution in Accordance with Income Classification in 1980 (in percentages)

Income classification	Percentage	Cumulative Percentage
Total	100.0	
–39 ten thousand yen	0.7	0.7
40–59	1.4	2.1
60–79	2.2	4.3
80–99	2.7	7.0
100–119	2.6	9.6
120–139	3.2	12.8
140–159	3.2	16.0
160–179	3.2	19.2
180–199	3.3	22.5
200–239	8.3	30.7
240–279	9.3	40.0
280–319	9.2	49.2
320–359	8.3	57.4
360–399	6.9	64.3
400–499	14.1	78.4
500–599	8.9	87.3
600–699	4.6	91.6
700–799	2.7	94.5
800–899	1.7	96.3
900–999	1.1	97.3
1000–	2.7	100.0

Source: Ministry of Welfare Department of Statistics and Information, Report of the Survey of National Life, 1980.

FIGURE I

Cumulative Percentage of the Family Distribution by Income Classification

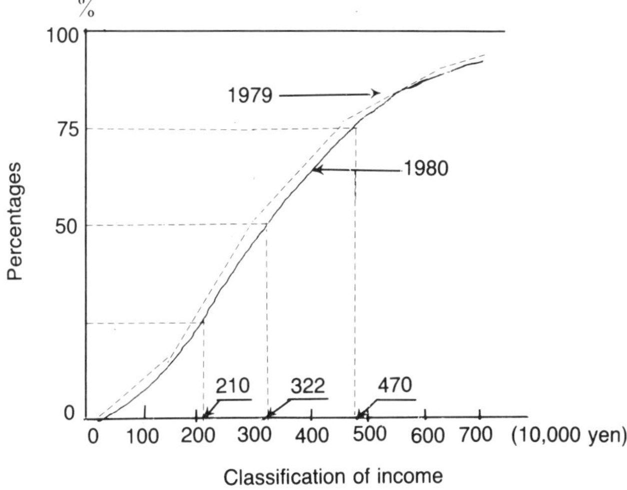

Source: Ministry of Welfare, Department of Statistics and Information, Report of the Survey of National Life, 1980.

FIGURE II

Lorenz Curve of Income Distribution in Japan in 1963 and 1970

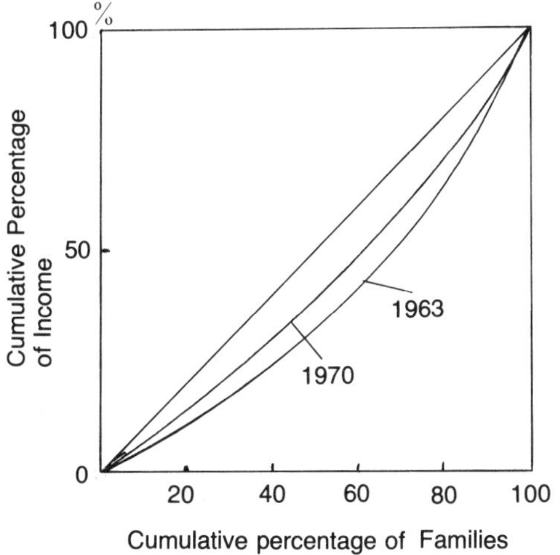

Source: Sueo Sekiguchi, *Nihon no Hinkon* (Poverty in Japan), Nihonkeizai Shimbun Co., Tokyo, 1976, p. 140.

22. It is widely believed among the Japanese, even by experts, that income distribution in Japan is generally more inequal than in the Western industrialised countries. However, scrupulous study of an international comparison of income distribution shows that although income distribution in Japan is more inequal than that in the Scandinavian countries, it is not very different from that in the United States, United Kingdom, West Germany or Holland (see Table VIII).

Another study of income distribution in the United States, Sweden, West Germany, East Germany, the United Kingdom and Japan even concludes that there is greater equality in the distribution of income in Japan than in the United States or West Germany.[1]

1. Martin Schnitzer, *Income Distribution, A comparative Study of the United States, Sweden, West Germany, the United Kingdom and Japan*, Praeger Publishers New York, 1974, p. 232.

23. One of the most important characteristics of the Japanese labour market is the difference in working conditions, including wages, according to the size

TABLE VIII

Classification of 9 countries according to the degree of inequality during 1965–8 (as judged by three criteria)

	Criterion of Inequality		
Degree of Inequality	High Proportion of Relatively Poor People	High Absorption of Income by the Well-To-Do	High Absorption of Income by the Rich
High	W. Germany 1965	W. Germany 1965 Japan 1968 USA 1967	W. Germany 1965 Japan 1968
Medium	Japan 1968 USA 1967 UK 1967	Holland 1966 UK 1967	USA 1967
Low	Holland 1966 Sweden 1968 Australia 1967–8 Norway 1967 Denmark 1967–8	Sweden 1968 Australia 1967–8	UK 1967 Holland 1966 Sweden 1968
Very Low		Norway 1967 Denmark 1967–8	Australia 1967–8 Norway 1967 Denmark 1967–8

From D. G. Champernowne, *The Distribution of Income between Persons*, Cambridge University Press, 1973, p. 42.

of the enterprise. Until the 1960's, employees working in small enterprises with less than 30 employees (who made up about 40 per cent of the total number of employed persons at that time) had been receiving less than half the amount of wages received by those working in larger enterprises with more than 500 employees (see Table X). However, because of the severe labour shortage in the late 1960's and early 1970's, working conditions in the smaller enterprises have improved steadily and considerably. In 1975 the wage level in the small enterprises had risen to nearly 70 per cent of that in the larger enterprises. However, this trend stopped and then started to decline gradually as shown in Table X.

§7. Social and Cultural Values

24. As a rare example of a country which has successfully married Western culture and an indigenous traditional culture, Japan has retained such traditional social values as respect for the aged, diligence, sensibility and modesty, and combined them with such modern democratic ideas as the freedom of the individual as well as of the enterprise, the guarantee of fundamental human rights and the democratic principle of distributing state power between the legislature, the executive and the judiciary. Moreover, the Japanese Constitution of 1946 not only established the guarantee of the basic human right of freedom of the individual against the state power, but it also introduced so-called 'social' human rights such as the right to existence, the right to work and the right of workers to organise. As well as this, the Constitution provides that standards for working conditions should be fixed by law. Thus, the Constitution of Japan proclaims the principle of a welfare state, obliging the Government to guarantee a certain standard of living for the people in general and equal labour standards for the workers.

25. Art. 28 of the Constitution establishes the foundations of collective labour law by guaranteeing the right to organise, to bargain collectively and to act collectively for all workers; while Art. 27, which requires the fixing of labour standards by law, lays the foundations of protective labour law. Such a constitutional guarantee of the workers' basic rights has provided a strong base for the development and growing influence of the trade union movement. However, in reality, this legal system of industrial relations is altered by the actual situation in Japanese industrial relations. Industrial relations in Japan are governed by three distinctive characteristics: the life-time employment system, the 'seniority' wage system and enterprise unionism.[1]

1. Each of these three characteristics of Japanese industrial relations will be discussed in its respective section: life-time employment in Part I, Chapter I, §1; seniority wages in Chapter IV, §4; and enterprise unionism in Part II, Chapter II, §1.

26. All of these characteristics play a part in promoting the loyalty of employees towards their enterprises, the flexibility of the labour force with regard to technological change and the co-operation of the unions with the

TABLE IX

Non-Agricultural Employment in the Private Sector by size of enterprise except government employees (in 1981)

Size of Enterprise	Number (thousand)	Percentage of Employees
1 to 29 employees	15,327	47.7
30 to 99	7,334	22.8
100 to 499	5,923	18.4
500 or more	3,549	11.0
Total private sector	32,132	100.0
Public corporations and public enterprises	3,663	(10.2)
Total employees in non-agricultural industries, except government employees	3,795	(100)

Source: Bureau of Statistics, Office of the Prime Minister, Statistical Survey of Enterprises, 1981.

TABLE X

Wage difference index by size of enterprise (total cash payment)

Size of Enterprise	1955	1960	1965	1970	1975	1980	1982
500 or more employees	100.0	100.0	100.0	100.0	100.0	100.0	100.0
100 to 499	74.3	70.7	80.9	81.4	82.9	80.5	78.9
30 to 99	58.8	58.9	71.0	69.6	68.7	65.4	64.1
5 to 29	–	46.3	63.2	61.8	60.2	58.0	56.7

Source: Monthly Labour Statistics Survey.

efforts of management. Thus, the Japanese industrial relations system has, on the whole, had the effect of stimulating economic growth and technological advancement in the post-war period; although it has also allowed some minor problems to arise, particularly in the field of small enterprises, which have been caused mainly by partial recessions.

27. State intervention through protective labour law certainly played an important part, especially in the early post-war period, in protecting workers' interests amid economic confusion. The right to organise, and collective labour law, have contributed to the rapid growth of union organisation and have given official authorisation and great influence to the unions which had been denied a legal existence during World War II. Today the unions enjoy a fairly important position within society, partly because of the comparative underdevelopment of other civil organisations and the weakness of the opposition parties. However, in the years since the oil crisis they have had to face a serious challenge. Now that the time of rapid economic growth and prosperity is over, the promotion of social justice by means of a more equitable distribution of income and wealth is being emphasised; as is the elimination of the strains caused by the too-rapid economic growth of the past, such as pollution and other public nuisances. Thus not only the large enterprises, but also the unions, both of which have enjoyed the fruits of the rapid economic growth, have begun to be criticised. The social responsibility of such organisations is to be stressed more in the future.

28. In the face of these new challenges the principle of free collective bargaining is to be re-examined, with the possibility of protecting those who have not been enjoying the fruits of economic growth in mind. Unions should be more ready to participate in policy-making to improve the welfare and security of those workers whose interests have been neglected in the past and who have, in effect, been sacrificed to the strains caused by rapid economic growth and prosperity. Protective labour law should be amended so as to protect those who have been exposed to danger as a result of technological development. More emphasis should be put on job security, given the increasing threat of unemployment both at the present time and in the future due to the shift in the economy from rapid growth to steady growth. Participation by workers and consumers in the management of the public sector and public utilities, as well as in the formation of industrial policy, should be encouraged. So, the general trend will be for Japanese industrial relations to become more tripartite and welfare-oriented.

II. Definitions and Notions

29. Social law or social legislation in Japan consists of labour law on the one hand and social security law on the other. However, the distinction between these two fields of law has never been very clear; although the former aims to protect workers or employees with regard to their working conditions, while the latter aims to promote the general standard of living of all the people. Especially in recent years, some legislation which had been regarded as a part of labour law – such as workmen's compensation – has extended its protection to cover accidents on the way to work. Also, protection which had hitherto been given only to employees is now often going to be extended to cover non-employed workers. Thus the general trend is to make the traditional demarcation more obscure and obsolete.

§1. Social Security Law

30. The social security system is divided into two categories: social insurance and social assistance. The former is financed by contributions from employers and employees or the self-employed, plus a Government subsidy, and is administered by the Ministry of Labour (in the case of employee insurance) or by the Ministry of Health and Welfare. The latter is mostly (80 per cent) subsidised by the national Government, with the remaining 20 per cent being subsidised by local government, and is administered by the local Welfare Offices. The social security system in general is complicated and confused by its division into various categories according to the status of the insured person and the nature of the accident, which for mainly historical reasons are administered by different agencies and provide unequal benefits for beneficiaries.

31. Social insurance is basically divided into an occupational scheme for employees of public and private institutions and a scheme for all those without employment status, which includes the self-employed, students and so on. The former scheme is divided into Health Insurance, Seamen's Insurance, Day-Labourers' Health Insurance, Employees' Pension Insurance, Workmen's Accident Compensation Insurance and Employment Insurance. The latter scheme includes National Health Insurance, National Pension, Farmers' Pension and Child Allowances.

32. In most of the occupational insurance schemes the cost of the benefits is covered by contributions from employees, employers and the Government in roughly the same proportions. With regard to Workmen's Accident Compensation and Child Allowances, the contributions are paid by the employers and the Government alone. In some of the social security programmes for those other than employees the contributions are collected from the insured persons, but in most of them the Government finances the whole cost. The administrative costs of all the social security programmes are taken care of by the national Government, with subsidies from local government in some cases. Table XI will show how much the social security system has expanded in recent years, taking the example of the share of health insurance coverage in the nation's medical care expenses. Remembering the minor role played by private medical insurance in Japan, one can claim that today nearly 85 per cent of medical expenses are covered by the social security system.

TABLE XI

Share of Medical Expenses

	1955	1965	1975	1980
Total amount (1,000 million Yen)	238.8	1,112.4	6,477.9	11,980.5
Average annual per head expenses (Yen)	2,675	11,421	57,900	102,500
SHARES:		(in per cents)		
National & local government	11.7	13.1	13.1	12.3
Insurance coverage	49.6	66.3	74.0	76.7
Patients	38.7	20.6	12.9	11.0

Source: International Society for Educational Information, *Japan Today*, Tokyo, 1976, 1983.

33. In total, the social security system provides a variety of benefits: medical care benefits, sickness and injury allowances for the insured and their dependants, delivery expenses for the insured and their spouses, maternity allowances, funeral expenses for the insured and their dependants, a survivor's pension, an invalidity pension and a retirement pension (or an old-age pension in the case of non-employees). The total amount of such public welfare costs makes up 6.1 per cent of total labour costs. The social assistance programme aims to guarantee a minimum standard of living for all those who cannot enjoy the various benefits under the social insurance system and provides seven types of assistance: livelihood assistance to help to buy the daily necessities (Y143,345 per month for a four person family in a large city in 1982) and assistance with medical expenses, children's education, housing, maternity, occupational training and funeral services.

34. As we have already mentioned, there are differences in the level of benefits provided for different categories of insured persons under the social security system. In general, the insurance scheme for employees provides better benefits than the scheme for non-employees, and the one for public employees provides better benefits than the one for private employees. (Table XII illustrates such differences in the amount of benefits of various schemes taking for example the pensions for retired or aged persons.) One has also to take into account the fact that most of the larger companies are providing additional benefits under the social security system for their employees as part of a very well developed company welfare system. This system provides extensive privileges for their employees such as clinic, hospital, resort and recreational facilities, educational facilities, education grants for employees' children, dormitories, housing facilities, retirement allowances in a lump sum (as distinguished from pensions) and so on.

TABLE XII

Amount of Pensions (per person and per year in yen) in the Different Schemes in 1981

Private employees	1,299,978
Seamen	1,765,900
National Government employees	1,675,462
Local Government employees	1,872,700
Public Corporations employees	1,822,189
Private school teachers	1,406,955
Non-employees	292,566

Source: Prime Minister's Office, Annual Report of Social Security Statistics.

§2. LABOUR LAW

35. Labour law can be regarded as the law which governs the relationship between employers and employees who provide labour in a position of *subordination* in accordance with the German notion of 'Abhängigkeit'. Thus, labour law does not apply to *independent labour* such as that done by the self-employed. The distinction is based on the civil law distinction between a contract of employment on the one hand and a contract of commission or trust on the other. So the same work done, for instance, by a carpenter will be covered by labour law if he is employed by a construction company to do it, whereas it will be not covered by labour law if he merely works under a contract with a customer. The same applies to the work done by artists, craftsmen, lawyers, and doctors. Although the Courts have been relying on the orthodox principle of *subordination*, according to which the degree of discretion allowed to the worker and the power to order allowed to the other party is crucial, legal precedents have tended to expand the protection of labour law so as to cover actual subordinate labour, regardless of the token form of the contract and taking into account the reality of the situation. For instance, in the case of the artist who had no formal employment contract with the broadcasting or television companies, the Court applied labour law.

36. Labour law is thus a body of legal norms governing the relationship between employers and the employees who provide them with labour and who in turn receive wages from them. In Japan, labour law applies to all employees as a matter of principal, regardless of the nature of their employer or the work they do. It applies not only to blue-collar workers but also to white-collar workers and public employees, including civil servants. Although very different rules are applied to employees in the public sector, especially in the field of collective labour law, these rules are regarded as exceptional restrictions on their rights as workers which can be justified only because of their special status and the necessity of avoiding public inconvenience. Thus, Japanese labour law is divided into the labour law of the private sector which is its usual pattern and the labour law of the public sector which is a deviation from basic principles (the notion of private and public sectors will be explained in §3, Categories of employee). Besides this division of labour law, the more important division is that between *individual labour law and collective labour law* – as is the case in many other countries.

I. Individual Labour Law

37. Individual labour law has its constitutional basis in Art. 27, Sec. 2 of the 1946 Constitution of Japan, which provides that standards for wages, hours, rest and other working conditions shall be fixed by law. Apart from this constitutional requirement, individual relations between employers and employees are governed by the civil law rules on contracts of employment; although these rules are modified considerably by labour law principles in order to protect employees and improve their working conditions. Thus, individual labour law can be described as the body of rules concerned with the individual relationship between employers and employees.

38. Individual labour law is, therefore, concerned with
- *the different categories of employees*: blue-collar versus white-collar, private versus public, regular versus temporary, seamen . . .;
- *the individual contract of employment*: form and content, the legal capacity to conclude contracts;
- *the rights and duties* of the parties in the course of the employment relationship;
- *working time, rest, holidays, annual vacation* and so on;
- *remuneration*;

- the rules concerning *incapacity to work*: due to illness, an accident at work, election to a full-time union post and so on;
- *job security*;
- *protection against discrimination*;
- *competition by former employees*;
- *inventions by employees*;
- settlement of *individual disputes*.

II. Collective Labour Law

39. Collective labour law has its constitutional basis in Art. 28 of the Constitution which guarantees to workers the rights to organise, bargain and act collectively. Since these workers' rights are regarded as fundamental human rights which are inviolable and cannot be infringed by legislation, all laws which promote them can be seen as confirmation and materalisation of the constitutional position. Thus, for instance, the provisions of the Trade Union Law of 1949 which provide legal protection for the unions and their rights to act (including the rights to bargain and to strike), and which give normative legal effect to any collective agreements, are regarded as confirming the consitutional principle. In other words, more or less the same legal effects would stem directly from the above-mentioned constitutional provisions, at least in so far as their substance is concerned. At the same time, if the law was ever amended in the future so as to deny these constitutional guarantees, such an amendment would be deemed unconstitutional and declared null and void by the Courts.

40. Collective labour law is concerned with collective labour relations, which includes such subjects as
- *trade union freedom* or the *right to organise*;
- *relationship between trade unions and employers or their associations* at plant, enterprise, industrial as well as at national level;
- *collective bargaining*
- *labour disputes*, including strikes and lock-outs
- *settlement of labour disputes and the protection of essential needs*.

III. Legal Nature

41. Japanese labour law can be regarded, in general, as having an '*imperative*' nature, since both individual and collective labour law has its consitutional foundation in the respective provisions of the Constitution which guarantee workers' rights as fundamental human rights. The Constitution regards these fundamental rights as inviolable and unalterable by agreement of the parties; as long, that is, as they aim to protect the workers in view of their unequal position in relation to the employers. In individual labour law, most of the provisions of the Labour Standards Law of 1947 provide minimum standards for working conditions. Individual as well as collective agreements setting lower standards are null and void, and employers can be punished by fines or imprisonment for violating most of the provisions of the Labour Standards Law. In collective labour law, the Trade Union Law admits the superiority of collective bargaining by giving normative legal effect to collective agreements. This means that any individual contract or work rule which contravenes the provisions of a collective agreement is *null and void* (Art. 16). Also, any agreement, including a collective one, which infringes the fundamental human rights of workers as guaranteed by the Constitution is null and void, since such constitutional guarantees are interpreted as having established *public order* with respect to workers' rights. For instance, yellow-dog contracts in which an employee promises to refrain from joining a union or to secede from a union as a condition of employment, or which allow the dismissal of an employee because of union activities or union membership, are interpreted as being null and void.

42. At the same time, the Trade Union Law prohibits as unfair labour practices the employer's discriminatory treatment of his employees because of their union membership or union activities, his refusal to bargain collectively and any interference by him in the formation or administration of trade unions. The Labour Relations Commission will investigate the case at the request of the union or the workers, and can accordingly issue orders which may include an order to reinstate a worker, to bargain in good faith or to cease and desist from interference. All these orders are enforceable with penalties (for a more detailed description, see Part II, Chapt. VI). Thus, the jurisdictions of the Courts and the Labour Relations Commissions overlap when the unfair labour practices take the form of legal action, as in the case of dismissal. However, it is generally agreed that there is, in fact, no real overlap. The Courts judge only the legal nature of the employer's action and declare whether or not it is illegal and therefore null and void; while the Commissions estimate the case from the administrative point of view to protect and encourage union activities and order the appropriate measures without paying any attention to, or even touching on, the legal effect of the action.

43. As we have already stated, the constitutional guarantees of the rights of workers are regarded as fundamental human rights and thus constitute *public policy*. This assertion, which has been overwhelmingly supported by almost all labour law scholars, has raised the difficult legal problem of the constitutionality of certain provisions to restrict the right to organise, to bargain and especially to strike in the public sector. More fundamentally, this problem poses the general question of how far workers' rights should be restricted in order to protect public welfare and convenience, and whether the restriction should be used only in emergencies or should be permitted, for instance, merely to protect or promote Government finances. (Such problems will be discussed in detail in their relevant sections later in this monograph, especially in Part II, Chapter V.)

§3. Categories of Employees

44. In Japan today, the distinction between blue-collar and white-collar workers is almost irrelevant, at least legally speaking. And the traditional distinction between these two categories which had been important both in terms of social status and also within enterprises in the pre-war period is now fading away rapidly, partly because labour law does not recognise any distinction in its field of jurisdiction and partly because of the efforts of individual enterprises to abolish most of the differences in working conditions. The more important distinction in Japanese daily employment relationships is now the one between *regular (permanent) employees* and *temporary employees*, which bears no relation to the distinction between white-collar and blue-collar workers. Regular employees, both white-collar and blue-collar, are those who are employed by the employer with an indefinite term contract and who are expected to stay in the enterprise until they reach retirement age, usually somewhere between 55 and 60. They are recruited on the basis of an annual intake of university and school leavers. Temporary employees, again both manual and office employees, can also be recruited fresh from school, but more often they have already worked in other enterprises. They are either employed for a definite or an indefinite term. But even if they are employed for an indefinite term, neither of the parties expect that they will stay in the enterprise for long and they are not recognised as having permanent status. However, quite often temporary employees do stay in the enterprise for a considerable period of time, and they may eventually be promoted to regular status at the discretion of the employer. The distinction is not a legal one, since temporary employees who are employed for an indefinite term are given the same protection regarding dismissal. But, in practice, temporary employees are the first to be dismissed whenever the enterprise has a labour surplus. They act as a kind of shock-absorber to cope with normal business fluctuation, since the regular employees who are employed for a life-time are an inflexible labour force. Regular employees enjoy job security, guaranteed steady advancement in rank and wages, the required training for a given job and finally, *a generous sum as a retirement allowance*. Temporary employees do not usually enjoy such privileges and often they are not even entitled to use company welfare facilities. Thus, temporary employees are an essential ingredient of the life-time employment system but are second-class citizens compared with regular employees, being the last hired and the first fired. Although in recent years, partly because of the labour shortage and partly because of demands for equality, some enterprises have promoted some of their temporary employees to regular status and there has been a growing tendency to employ those who have already worked for other enterprises as regular employees, it is still the case in most of the larger enterprises and in many of the smaller and medium-sized enterprises that the life-time employment system has a steady base and the difference in status and working conditions between regular and temporary employees continues to exist.[1]

1. The percentage of the various types of temporary employees, including part-time workers,

and working students, among the total employees in 1981 was 12.7 per cent (Ministry of Labour, Summary of Labour Statistics, Tokyo, 1983, p. 66).

45. Another important distinction between categories of employee stems from the nature of the employer. The major distinction is between private and public; while the public sector itself is also divided into different categories. This distinction is of a much more legal nature, since for each of the different categories there are applied different laws based on different principles – especially in connection with the right to organise, to bargain and to strike. The Trade Union Law applies to the employees of all private employers and most of the minor public corporations. The Public Corporation and National Enterprise Labour Relations Law of 1948 (PCNELR) covers labour relations in three major public corporations (National Railways, Telegraph and Telephone Public Corporation and the Japan (Tobacco) Monopoly Public Corporation) and four national government enterprises [Post, State-owned Forests, Printing (of bank-notes, postage stamps etc.) and Minting (coins)]. The Local Public Enterprise Labour Relations Law of 1952 (LPELR) applies to employees in local government enterprises such as local railways, tramways, automobile transportation, gas and water supply. The National Civil Service Law of 1947 and the Local Civil Service Law of 1950 cover, respectively, the national and local government employees who are not covered by the above-mentioned laws governing public enterprises. In other words, the *Civil Service Law* is applied to almost all employees in Government offices, including high ranking civil servants.

46. Table XIII shows the number of employees covered by different laws. One can see that the organisation rate in the public sector, except in the national civil service, is very high in comparison to that in the private sector. This is partly explained by the fact that the public corporations are larger enterprises; and is related to the fact that in the private sector the organisation rate in the larger enterprises is close to the rate in public corporations, whereas in the smaller enterprises it is quite low and there are often no unions at all – especially in enterprises with less than 50 employees. The high organisation rate in the local civil service is explained by the fact that teachers in public schools are very well organised.

§4. Leading Personnel – Supervisors

47. Leading personnel, supervisors, and even top managers – as long as they are not on the board of directors of their company – are regarded as workers under Japanese labour law. They are covered by the whole range of protective labour law. However, at the same time, they are regarded as 'employers' under the Labour Standards Law in as far as their role is to 'act on behalf of the owner of the enterprise in matters concerning the workers in the enterprise' (Art. 10). This definition extends the notion of 'employers' to cover those who actually carry out the daily business of personal management. Their acts are regarded as having been done by the employer and the liability for these actions is attributable to the employer. Both of them are subject to penal sanctions.

TABLE XIII

Number of Employees and Organisation Rate by Applicable Labour Laws, 1983

(unit: 10,000 people)

Applicable Labour Laws	Total	Organised Labour: Number of Employees	Organised Labour: Organisation rate	Unorganised and non-eligible employees
Trade union Law	3,582	905	25.3	2,677
Public Sector	520	348	66.9	172
PCNELR Law	115	97	84.3	18
LPELR Law	25[1]	23	92.0	2
National Civil Service	84	29	34.5	55
Ordinary	50	29	58.0	21
Special[2]	34	—	—	34
Local Civil Service	296	199	67.2	97
Ordinary	259	199	76.2	60
Special[2]	37	—	—	37
Total number of Employees	4,102	1,253	30.5	2,849

Source: Ministry of Labour, *Basic Survey of Trade Unions, Labour Force Survey*; Personnel Authority, *Survey on Wages of National Civil Service*; Ministry of Autonomous Governing Bodies, *Survey on Employees' Organisations etc.*

1. Number of employees of local public enterprises and employed for simple labour except those who are organised by one of the local civil service organisations.
2. Policemen, firemen, prison workers, civil defence personnel who are not permitted to organise.

48. The Trade Union Law also disqualifies from registration those unions which admit as members 'workers at the supervisory level having direct authority to hire, fire, promote or transfer, workers at the supervisory level having access to confidential information relating to the employer's labour relations plans and policies so that their official duties and obligations directly conflict with their loyalties and obligations as members of the trade union concerned and other persons who represent the interests of the employer' (Art. 2(1)).

III. Historical Background

§1. The Pre-War Period

49. Japanese industry developed early in the 20th century as a result of the victory in the war against Russia. The war effort brought prosperity to heavy industry especially. Not only the number of factories and workers, but also the scope of the factories, increased rapidly; both during and after the war. This trend necessitated the provision and maintenance of a modern labour force, and its protection. Thus, in 1911, came the Factory Law, the first piece of labour legislation to be introduced in Japan. However, it concentrated mainly on providing protection for female and child labour, and even this protection was very timid. For instance, the maximum number of working hours per day for women and children was 12 (later to be made 11 by the Amendment of 1923) and the enforcement of the prohibition of night work was postponed for 15 years after its introduction. The only protection provided for adult male workers was compensation for accidents at work. As well as the Factory Law, a protective law for seamen and an order to protect miners (a 10-hour working day) were introduced.

50. The development of legislation in the field of collective labour relations was even more miserable. Several efforts made before the 2nd World War to introduce a trade union law proved unsuccessful. The first draft of the Trade Union Law was submitted to the Diet in 1921, and after that for a few years almost every session of the Diet had similar drafts pending but never passed them. Instead, in 1926, the Labour Dispute Mediation Law was passed. This law provided a mediation service for settling labour disputes, and in particular introduced a system of compulsory mediation for public utility work such as transportation. It also prohibited the inducement and instigation of acts of dispute during the mediation process. After 1930 the emerging militarism made it impossible to pass any trade union law. The beginning of the war against China in 1937, and then the 2nd World War, completely denied the possibility of any developments in labour law until the end of the war. In 1940 the Military Government ordered the then-existing unions to join the *Sangyō Hōkoku Kai* (Industrial Association to Serve the State), which was the Japanese version of the *Arbeitsfront* of Nazi Germany.

51. Outside labour legislation, some of the provisions of the criminal law were used to suppress the union movement and especially to prevent strikes. The most notorious was Article 17 of the Peace Police Act of 1900 which prohibited inducement and instigation to organise unions or collective action, and so virtually suppressed almost all union activity. Thus, while organising unions was not of itself prohibited, and perhaps even theoretically protected by the guarantee of freedom of association in the 1889 Constitution of the Empire of Japan, those who actually tried to organise were arrested and punished by the Peace Police Act. The Order to Punish Minor Crimes and local police orders had the same effect. Although Article 17 of the Peace Police Act was abolished in 1926, another law called the Act to Penalise Violence etc. was introduced in the same session of the Diet. This Act was often applied to union activities, especially if violence was involved. The Peace Preservation Act of 1925 was also used against the unions, and in particular against those with a radical idiology.

52. The underdevelopment of labour law in pre-war Japan can be best explained by the weakness of the trade unions and of the political parties which represented the working classes. The Japanese economy, to which industrialisation came late, found it necessary to depend on cheap labour, longer working hours and other poor working conditions in order to compete with the already-developed economies of the Western world. The ruling political forces represented the interests of businessmen, landowners and bureaucrats. The unions and the political parties which represented the working classes were not only weak, but also suffered from repeated splits and confrontations between small factions within themselves. These splits in the union organisations caused by ideological commitment, as well as being characteristic of the pre-war union movement, still to some extent regulate the character of the union movement, and as a result the character of industrial relations, in Japan today.

53. The influence of organised labour in the pre-war period was very limited. The highest organisation rate (the percentage of organised workers among the total number of employed persons) in pre-war Japan was 7.9 in 1931; the number of unions being 818 and the number of organised workers 369,000. In addition to the small number of organised workers, the union organisations suffered from ideological strife between unions and especially between their leaders. In a social and political climate antagonistic towards the union movement unionism tended to be associated with the political movements of anarcho-syndicalism, socialism and communism. Serious confrontations and rivalry between these political groups brought about splits between the union organisations connected with the respective political factions. A split between the parties immediately resulted in a union split and vice versa. The ideological differences between the union organisations helped to weaken a union movement which was not very influential to begin with. Thus, taken together, the antagonistic social and political climate, the legal setting and the weakness of the unions' influence caused by their poor organisation and the splits between them hardly made for the development of sound trade unionism or indeed for the development of a modern labour law system based on such trade unionism. After the 2nd World War the peculiar political situation created by the policy of the Occupation Forces meant that a modern labour law system was suddenly born. But the characteristics of the pre-war labour movement were mostly inherited by the post-war union movement, and they prescribed its fundamental nature. These elements still cannot be neglected if we are to understand present-day Japanese industrial relations and labour law enforcement.

§2. Post-War Industrial Relations

I. The Formation of Enterprise Unionism

54. As soon as the Allied Occupation Forces arrived in Japan they began to encourage the formation of unions as one of the means of democratising Japanese society. Strong unionism was regarded as the best counteraction to the influence of big business, which together with the military leadership, was presumed to have led Japan into war. Leading figures, including the owners of businesses and high-ranking managers, were in a weak position, having lost their goal. Thus, it was quite a rare situation in the history of the world labour movement that workers wishing to form unions faced no objections either from the Government or from the employers. If there is no resistance to unionisation it is quite natural and most convenient for the workers to start their organising efforts within the enterprises,where most workers already are. They need not go to the trouble of gathering somewhere in town after work, often in secret in order to avoid the attention of the employers or even of the police, which has usually been the case with regard to the formation of unions in other countries. This is one of the historical reasons why, after the 2nd World War, unions were organised within enterprises. Quite often thy were organised under the leadership of the Occupation Forces or the Japanese Government, the latter willingly obeying the policy of the former.

55. The economic dilapidation and confusion shortly after the War also provided fertile ground for the emergence of unionism. Thus, within 10 years of the end of the War the unions were organising more than six million workers, the organisation rate having reached 35 per cent.

II. The Function of Enterprise Unions

56. In 1982 there were about 74,000 unions organising more than 12 million workers, which is nearly 30 per cent of all employed persons. In 1980, 94 per cent of all the unions which cover about 90 per cent of organised labour were enterprise unions. Thus today, with a few exceptions – including the Seamen's Union as the most important one, and some general unions mainly organising small shops and factories where the establishment of enterprise unionism is hardly to be expected on a district basis – the overwhelming majority of unions organise employees in a particular enterprise or in a particular plant. In these enterprise unions, being an employee of the particular enterprise is a prerequisite for union membership. Those who have lost the status of employee will also lose union membership, unless the union is challenging the legality of the dismissal.

57. Enterprise unions are often suspected, especially by Westerners, of being too dependent on management; and they are undoubtedly more co-operative, if not more loyal, than industrial unions. Their bargaining power must inevitably be limited by their natural tendency to consider the financial position of their own enterprise and the competitive situation with regard to rival companies, since their very existence depends on the existence and well-being of the enterprise. Admitting the shortcomings of enterprise unionism, some of the national centres of the trade unions have, for more than 20 years, been emphasising the strengthening of industrial unionism and the overcoming of enterprise unionism. But none of these efforts has added up to any significant change.

58. The peculiar historical situation immediately after the War only explains why enterprise unionism developed in the first place; but one may, with good reason, wonder why enterprise unionism still exists and functions. The answer is that it is still the most suitable type of union organisation for protecting the interests of Japanese workers. Under the life-time employment system the fate of regular employees, who make up the majority of Japanese employees, depends on how much they can get from the particular enterprise in which they have been employed throughout their working lives. Since they do not expect to move from one enterprise to another, working conditions in other companies are of no concern to them. The standard wage level in a certain industry in a certain district would only be of concern to those workers who might eventually move within this sector – which happened to be the case in Western society when the craft unions were organised. Given that the worker expects to stay in a particular enterprise until retirement, he will prefer to be protected by the union which bargains exclusively with the employer about working conditions in the particular enterprise.

III. Industrial Unions and National Centres

59. Thus, collective bargaining is mainly carried out at enterprise level; that is, between the employer and the union in the particular enterprise. However, most of the enterprise unions are affiliated to industrial federations. Industrial unions in Japan are mostly federations of enterprise unions in a certain industry. The only significant exception in the Seamen's Union which organises seamen regardless of the enterprise in which they work. Among the industrial federations, the most important are those covering the private railways, steel, metal and engineering, chemicals, textiles, shipbuilding and automobiles. Most of the unions in the public sector are organised on an enterprise basis; namely one for each public corporation or government enterprise, with a few exceptions such as the Teachers' Union and the Municipal Workers' Union.

60. These industrial federations and some of the more important enterprise unions, especially the larger ones in the public sector, are directly affiliated to the national centre. There are four major national centres, of which two are more important in terms of membership and influence. One is the *Sōhyō* (General Council of Trade Unions of Japan) which organised 50 unions and federations covering 4½ million members in 1982. Another is the Dōmei

(Japanese Confederation of Labour) which organised 32 unions and federations with 2.2 million members in the same year. Besides these national centres, the Japanese Council of Metalworkers' Unions (IMF–JC), which has affiliated with the International Metalworkers' Federation, has been gaining influence in recent years. Together they organise unions in metal and related industries, regardless of their affiliation to the national centres; and in 1982 they covered nearly 2 million workers. The Sōhyō has had the most dominant influence in the post-war labour movement, and politically it has been closely connected with the Japanese Socialist Party. The Dōmei, on the other hand, has had close contact with the Democratic Socialist Party. The division of the unions into national centres has been mainly for ideological reasons, with differences in industrial relations policy being less defined – although the Sōhyō has been more radical or demanding while the Dōmei has been more moderate. Over the last 10 years the Sōhyō has been gradually losing its influence, especially in the private sector. As a matter of fact at present the Dōmei organises more workers than the Sōhyō, at least as far as the private sector is concerned (see Table XIV).

Thus the Sōhyō's sphere of influence is now in the public sector, where political activities are still important because of the very nature of the sector and especially because of the pending political problem about the right of public employees to strike (see Part II, Chapter V).

IV. Recent Changes and Developments

61. The main reason for *the decline of the Sōhyō* in the private sector is to be found in the changing attitude of workers towards working life and society in general. One of the most significant contributions which the Sōhyō has made to Japanese industrial relations is the introduction of '*shuntō*' (the spring offensive). This tactic was invented and introduced by the Sōhyō leaders about 20 years ago and was established as a scheme in its present form around 1960. This scheme is based on the idea that several unions in enterprises of more or less the same size or significance within a certain industry will co-ordinate their wage demands once a year, mostly in the late spring, arranging their schedule of bargaining with the individual employers and their strikes for the same period; all under the leadership of the industrial federations. Through such co-ordinated action, the Sōhyō hoped that they could avoid the unfavourable situation which results from enterprise bargaining; namely, only the unions in prosperous enterprises get higher wages and those in less prosperous ones have to accept lower wages. Today, the spring offensive has become established as a sort of annual event in which not only unions in the Sōhyō, but also independent unions and those affiliated to the Dōmei, participate. The industrial federations, various committees of the national centres and the industrial union leaders select target industries and fix the level of wage demands for each year. Unions in prosperous industries with a well-organised membership and strong leaders are selected as 'pattern setters'. The wages achieved by the leading negotiations in these industries often play a dominant

TABLE XIV

Distribution of Membership in Major National Centres by Applicable Labour Law (1982)

(unit: 1,000 persons)

Major National Centres	Total	Trade Union Law	Public Corporation & National Enterprise Labour Relations Law; Local Public Enterprise Labour Relations Law	National Public Service Law; Local Public Service Law
Total	12,526	9,046	1,195	2,284
Sōhyō	4,450	1,470	1,049	2,032
Dōmei	2,197	2,037	118	42
Shinsanbetsu	61	60	–	–
Churitsurōren	1,439	1,438	–	–
Others	4,691	4,451	28	211

Note: Since the union members affiliated to more than one national centre are counted twice, total union membership does not necessarily equal the total of the various categories.
Source: Basic Survey of Trade Unions, 1982, Ministry of Labour, Tokyo.

role in deciding the 'market price' of the amount of the wage-hike for the year, which is then followed roughly by the other industries.

62. In spite of its radical attitude in political arguments, and its dedication to organising political campaigns in the form of demonstrations and activating support for the Socialist Party in elections, the Sōhyō had been gaining influence among the workers; mainly because of its success in getting higher wages through the spring offensive. However, some economists have raised doubts about the effectiveness of the spring offensive as a means of getting higher wages, attributing the main reason for rising wage levels to the rapid growth of the Japanese economy and the acute labour shortage after 1960 instead. But there is no doubt that without the strong influence of the Sōhyō, and especially without the massive wave of strikes every year, Japanese workers could not have achieved today's high wage levels. However, the very results of economic development and higher wages have now started to work against the Sōhyō leadership. The conspicuous features of the affluent society have made their radical ideology and slogans, and their emphasis on political activities, more or less obsolete. The difference in political ideology is beginning to lose its significance. The reason for the growing influence of the IMF–JC and the trend towards a more bread-and-butter oriented policy, even among the Sōhyō affiliated union leaders, are both quite understandable from this point of view. For several years now, efforts to unify the divided organisations have been intensifying. As a result, *Zenmin Rōkyō* (Japanese Private Sector Trade Union Council), a tentative body to promote the unification of unions regardless of national affiliations, was established in 1982 to cover 4.8 million workers.

63. Unions in Japan, which are usually enterprise unions, tend to pay most attention to working conditions in individual enterprises. In spite of the radical political utterances of the union leaders arguing for the welfare of the working class, the unions have paid little attention to the well-being of members of society outside their organisations. As a matter of fact, most of the enterprise unions have limited their membership to regular employees only; thus denying temporary employees the chance of participating in the gains of union activities. After enjoying rapid economic growth for nearly 20 years Japanese society is now facing a new challenge: how to solve the problem of the evils caused by heavy industrialisation, which include pollution and an unequal distribution of wealth and welfare. Being enterprise unions the Japanese unions are facing a critical dilemma, one aspect of which is how to cope with the pollution problems caused by their enterprises while still enjoying the fruits of the activities of these enterprises. The unions are now required, together with the enterprises, to be responsible to society in general. The only reasonable way for the unions to do this is to participate more in management and industrial policy-making, instead of bargaining with the enterprises in the traditional way which protects the well-being of workers only as employees.

64. In Japan industrial relations within an enterprise are usually amicable, the employees having consideration for their employers and co-operating with their plans and the enterprise unions being enterprise-conscious and playing the game only within the limits which the interests of the enterprise will allow. However, this harmonious relationship is possible only when both parties feel that they share common interests; and so when employees become aware of a divergence in interests the harmonious relationship is destined to break down. Such cases arise, most typically, either when the employer decides to dismiss a number of employees (perhaps because there is a serious labour surplus), or when some of the employees feel dissatisfied with their treatment by the enterprise (maybe in the field of promotion). In practice most of the employees' grievances and dissatisfactions are taken care of by the management in an informal way, without resorting to formal procedures or applying any universal norms. Most conflicts are settled by mutual understanding without ever being raised in any explicit form. Thus, Japanese employers and managers are not used to overt confrontation and the logical settlement of conflicting interests. This means that there is a tendency in Japanese industrial relations, once a conflict has become explicit, for a settlement to be very hard to reach. In such cases the dispute tends to be prolonged, and may turn into a fierce confrontation which often involves violence. Apart from the political struggle led by some ideologically committed unions, most of the difficult disputes which make up the overwhelming number of labour disputes – excluding those in the spring offensive – are this type of dispute. Whether or not the numbers of such disputes will be reduced in future by the efforts to rationalise the channels of conflict resolution within the enterprise, and especially at workshop level, is yet to be seen. This is certainly another problem which remains for the Japanese unions to solve in the future.

IV. The Role of the Government

§1. The Autonomy of the Social Partners

65. The autonomy of the social partners has long been emphasised in Japanese industrial relations as being one of its major principles. In general, Government leadership in the field of business is fairly strong; especially with regard to finance, exports, imports and industrial development, including the development of new technologies. In contrast, in the field of industrial relations the Government has always been very careful to refrain from intervention; perhaps out of respect for the right of workers to bargain, rather than because of any respect for the freedom of business activities. The only exceptions are, of course, labour inspection to enforce the minimum standards set by the Labour Standards Act and other protective labour laws, and police intervention in criminal cases arising from labour disputes. However, the Japanese police are very cautious in this respect because of their notorious record in the pre-war period. They usually refuse to get mixed-up in labour disputes unless there has been violence or some serious crime is clearly involved. It is claimed that the Government interferes in wage determination, especially in the case of the spring offensive, through the conciliation and arbitration procedures of the Labour Relations Commissions. But since the public members of these commissions are appointed with the consent of both the employer members and the labour members, the Government hardly dares press them to accept Government policy against their will. However, after the oil crisis and given the general trends in a highly technological industrial society, the role of the Government in protecting not only organised workers but all the other members of society against the unequal distribution of welfare and danger to life and physical well-being in such fields as safety and environmental protection is expected to grow.

§2. Government Institutions

I. The Ministry of Labour

66. The Ministry of Labour is the Government institution which bears most responsibility for industrial relations and a part of social insurance. The Ministry has five major bureaux, namely; Labour Policy, Labour Standards, Women and Minors, Employment Security and Vocational Training. At the local level, the Ministry has Prefectural Labour Standards Offices and Women and Minors Offices in each prefecture, and Labour Standards Inspection Offices and Public Employment Security Offices in each district. With regard to social insurance, employment insurance and workmen's compensation insurance are taken care of by the Labour Ministry; while most of the rest of social insurance is under the charge of the Ministry of Welfare. Thus, the Ministry of Labour commands almost exclusive administrative authority in the field of industrial relations. Each prefectural government also has its own section of the Labour Policy Bureau and Labour Policy Offices, but in most cases their function is only educational and consultative – although they may conciliate some minor labour disputes.

II. Labour Inspection

67. The Labour Standards Bureau is responsible for labour inspection. Labour inspectors are appointed from those who have qualified by means of a special examination, and they are then given guaranteed security in their job. They are authorised to inspect working places and other facilities, to examine records and documents, to interrogate employers and employees and to exercise the right of a judicial police officer with regard to the crime of violating protective labour law.

III. The Labour Relations Commissions

68. There are three kinds of Labour Relations Commission. The Central Labour Relations Commission (CLRC) and the Local Labour Relations Commission (LLRC) cover labour relations in private industry and local public enterprises, while the Public Corporations and National Enterprise Labour Relations Commission (PCNELRC) covers labour relations in public corporations and Government enterprises under the PCNELRL. Seamen's labour relations are governed by the Seamen's Central Labour Relations Commission and the Seamen's Local Labour Relations Commissions. All these Commissions have two main functions which are of a very different nature; one is a semi-judicial function with regard to unfair labour practice cases, and the other concerns labour dispute settlement through conciliation, mediation and arbitration. The former function only covers complaints about discriminatory treatment, a refusal to bargain and interference in and dominance over union administration by the employers. Other complaints and disputes in the field of industrial relations will fall under the jurisdiction of the ordinary courts, since there is no labour court in Japan. (For a more detailed description of the functions of the Labour Relations Commissions, see Part II, Chapter VI and VII.)

V. Sources of Labour Law

§1. The Constitution

69. Articles 27 and 28 of the Constitution are regarded as being the most fundamental legal sources of labour law. Article 27, section 1 provides for the right to work, thus giving a constitutional basis to the legislation concerning security of employment – including employment exchange agencies, unemployment insurance and vocational training. Section 2 of Article 27 provides a basis for protective labour law in general by requiring the fixing of standards of working conditions by law. Section 3 of the same article prohibits the exploitation of children, thus providing a basis for the legislative protection of child labour. Article 28 guarantees the right of workers to organise, bargain and act collectively, which gives a constitutional basis to legislation in the field of collective industrial relations. The fact that these Constitutional provisions guarantee the rights of workers, and at the same time the Constitution provides that they should be defined by law 'in conformity with public welfare', gives us good reason for interpreting the spirit of the Constitution so as to ensure fairly favourable treatment of workers as against employers. Thus, it is believed, the very nature of the Constitution provides a favourable atmosphere for labour law in Japan.

§2. Legislation

70. Most of the major labour law legislation was enacted shortly after the 2nd World War and amended in the late 1950's or early 1960's to a certain degree. Since then it has suffered only minor, mostly technical amendments. This legislation includes the Trade Union Law, the Labour Relations Adjustment Law of 1946 and the Labour Standards Law, which are often called the three major labour laws. Some other laws have been introduced or have experienced major amendment, especially after 1970, in keeping with the changing situation in a highly technological industrialised society. Such laws include the Labour Safety and Hygiene Law of 1972, the Employment Measures Law of 1966, the Vocational Training Law of 1969, the Employment Insurance Law of 1974, the Workmen's Compensation Law of 1947, the Workers' Asset Building Promotion Law of 1971, the Law concerning the Guarantee of Wage Payment of 1976 and the Women Workers' Welfare Law of 1972. All these laws are applied generally to private employees and in part to public employees. Another group of laws cover only certain categories of employees; the most important laws in this group being the Seamen's Law of 1947 and the already-mentioned PCNELRL, LPELRL, National Civil Service Law and Local Civil Service Law.

71. Apart from the above-described statutes enacted by Parliament, the Minister of Labour and the Central Labour Relations Commission both issue orders (ordinances) and by-laws based on the statutes. These subsidiary laws have a validity that is inferior to that of the statutes. The Labour Ministry has issued numerous orders concerning the interpretation and implementation of each statute in the field of labour law. Of these, the most important are the Ordinance for the Enforcement of the Labour Standards Law, the Ordinances about the Labour Standards of Women and Minors and many ordinances and rules regarding the Labour Safety and Hygiene Law.

§3. Collective Agreements and Rules of Work

72. Collective agreements between the union and employer or employers' association have the effect of autonomous legal norms in Japan. The Trade Union Law provides that every individual contract or work rule which contravenes the standard of working conditions established by the collective agreement is null and void. Since of course collective agreements may not run counter to imperative legal provisions, a collective agreement is the second strongest legal norm. It is an autonomous norm in the sense that it is created by private parties and is, in principle, binding only on these parties and their members. However, the Trade Union Law admits that it has legal binding effect beyond this limitation under certain conditions. If three-quarters of the employees in a certain plant are covered by a collective agreement, the agreement is automatically extended to cover all the remaining employees – at least as far as working conditions are concerned. If the majority of workers of a similar kind in a certain locality come under the application of one collective agreement, it will be declared by the Labour Minister or the Prefectural Governor to extend to the remaining workers of the same kind in the locality, and their employers, in accordance with the resolution of the Labour Relations Commission. Work rules also acquire the nature of legal norms in relation to the individual contract. According to the Labour Standards Law, a labour contract stipulating conditions inferior to those fixed in the work rules is null and void. In industrial relations in Japan today the role of the individual contract is very limited, since the introduction of work rules is obligatory for employers who employ more than 10 employees continuously and about 24 per cent of all employed persons (75 per cent of organised workers) are covered by collective agreements.

73. However, given the strong legal effect of collective agreements and work rules, one can easily overestimate their actual function. Collective agreements and work rules only stipulate the fundamental rules of the labour relationship. It is often pointed out that, in general, Japanese collective agreements are both simple and vague, with fewer and less detailed provisions than Western ones. Thus, in Japanese industrial relations most of the rules of behaviour and the concrete rights and obligations of both parties are actually decided by the power relationship between the union and the employer; and also by the power structure at shop-floor level (for example, the relationship between the rank and file and the foremen).

§4. Cases and Legal Theories

74. There is no formal text in Japan stating whether legal decisions are a source of law or not, although there is a provision which states that the decision of a higher ranking court in a case is binding on the lower court to which that particular case is referred. In theory, no judge is bound by anything except the Constitution and the law, and he is free to decide independently according to his conscience. Thus, the notion of binding precedent or *stare decisis* is unknown in Japan. But, in practice, case law is important because the legislation tends to be rather abstract, prescribing only the fundamental rules, and so the case law is necessary to fill out the legislative provisions when new cases arise. It is clear, therefore, that for the study of law the study of legal precedents is inevitable. In labour law especially, with its short history (most of the legislation having been introduced only after the 2nd World War), case law has played a very important role. But at the same time this fact also leads to some confusion in the case law of labour law. Both the theory and practice of labour law is rather new and no significant established tradition exists, with the result that almost any legal argument can command respect. Young judges often tend to adopt new theories, and this trend causes instability in the case law. As for legal theory, Japanese law, in common with most other modern legal systems, does not recognise it as a legal source. However, the judges pay considerable attention to the work of legal scholars. Quite a few reviews of court decisions are published in a number of legal journals and they are usually carefully watched by the judges.

75. The orders and decisions of the Labour Relations Commissions have almost as much importance as decisions of the Courts; at least in the field of unfair labour practice cases.

§5. Custom and Practice

76. Feelings are divided as to whether or not customs in general are a source of law. However, it is generally accepted that customs which do not contradict imperative law or public order can be regarded as a source of law. Furthermore, in some cases the judges have in fact accepted customs which contradicted imperative laws. Such judgments are more or less justified because the judge is not so much required to apply the existing rules of law at any cost, but rather to give a reasonable solution to the parties actually before him. In labour law, custom is especially important because many of the theories and some of the decided cases admit that collective agreements can be made without writing, in spite of the provision in the Trade Union Law requiring the written form. As a result, customs which have been accepted without any explicit agreement can often be granted the same legal effect as collective agreements.

§6. INTERNATIONAL SOURCES

77. The Constitution is silent on the question of whether a signed and ratified international treaty has the value of law at national level, and legal theories are divided on this point. However, at least in the field of labour law, it is generally accepted that the ratified conventions of the ILO have legal effect at national level. To some extent they have acquired an importance second only to that of the Constitution itself. In several cases, including a few Supreme Court decisions, the Courts have declared or implied that a legislative provision which contravenes one of the ILO conventions is null and void. Once, Japan was notorious (especially before the 2nd World War) for her reluctance to ratify ILO conventions. As of 1983, Japan has ratified 37 ILO conventions, including such important ones as Nos. 87, 98 and 135 concerning freedom of association and the right to organise, but had not yet ratified some of the fundamental ones like Nos. 1, 30 or 47 concerning hours of work.

VI. Selected Bibliography[1]

§1. Industrial Relations and Social Background

78. Abegglen, J., *Management and Worker: the Japanese solution* (Tokyo: Sophia/Kodansha International, 1973).

Ballon, R. J. (ed.), *The Japanese Employee* (Tokyo: Sophia/Tuttle, 1969).

Cole, R. E., *Japanese Blue-Collar Workers* (Berkeley: University of California Press, 1973).

Cole, R. E., *Work, Mobility and Participation: A Comparative Study of American and Japanese Industry* (Berkeley: University of California Press, 1979).

Dore, R. P., *British Factory – Japanese Factory* (Berkeley: University of California Press, 1973).

Hanami, T., *Labour Relations in Japan Today* (Tokyo: Kodansha International, 1979).

Horke, G., *Arbeiter unter der roten Sonne – Japans Unternehmengewerkschaften* (Wien: Europaverlag, 1976).

Nakane, C., *Japanese Society* (Harmondsworth: Penguin Books Ltd., 1973).

Nakayama, I., *Industrialisation and Labour Management Relations in Japan* (Tokyo: Japanese Institute of Labour, 1975).

OECD, *The Development of Industrial Relations Systems – Some Implications of the Japanese Experience* (Paris: OECD, 1977).

Rohlen, T. P., *For Harmony and Strength* (Berkeley: University of California Press, 1975).

Shirai, T. (ed.), *Contemporary Industrial Relations in Japan* (Madison: University of Wisconsin Press, 1983).

§2. Law in General

79. Noda, Y., *Introduction to Japanese Law* (Tokyo: University of Tokyo Press, 1976).

Tanaka, H., *The Japanese Legal System – Introductory Cases and Materials* (Tokyo: University of Tokyo Press, 1976).

Von Mehren, A. T. (ed.), *Law in Japan* (Tokyo: Harvard/Tuttle, 1963).

3. Labour Law

I. Legislation

1. There are very few publications in any Western language on Japanese labour law, although in the general field of Japanese industrial relations a fair number of publications are now available in English. I have covered here only the important books on industrial relations (mostly published after 1970) and some of the articles on labour law. Readers will also find many useful articles on industrial relations and labour law in the *Japan Labour Bulletin*, which will aid their understanding of contemporary issues.

80. Ministry of Labour, *Japanese Labour Laws* (Tokyo: Ministry of Labour, 1980).

II. Articles

Hanami, T., 'The Characteristics of Labour Disputes in Japan' in *Social and Cultural Background of Labour – Management Relations in Asian Countries* (Tokyo: Japanese Institute of Labour, 1972).

Hanami, T., 'The Influence of ILO Standards on Law and Practice in Japan' in *International Labour Review*, Vol. 120, No. 6, November–December 1981.

Hanami, T., 'The Life-time Employment System in Japan' in *Atlanta Economic Review*, May–June, 1976.

Mitsufuji, T., and Hagisawa, K., 'Recent Trends in Collective Bargaining in Japan' in ILO, *Collective Bargaining in Industrialised Market Economies* (Geneva: ILO, 1974).

Nishimura, K., 'Labour Law' in Kitagawa, Z. (ed.), *Doing Business in Japan*, Vol. 6 (N.Y.: Methew Bender, 1981).

Tsukamoto, S. and Hanami, T., 'Contracts of Employment in Japan' in Aronstein, C. S., *International Handbook on Contracts of Employment* (Deventer, The Netherlands: Kluwer, 1976).

III. Periodicals

Japan Labour Bulletin, Japanese Institute of Labour, Tokyo.

Part I. The Individual Employment Relationship

Chapter I. Definitions and Concepts

§1. The Different Categories of Employees

81. The distinction between *blue-collar* and *white-collar* employees is less important, as we have already described, both in legal and industrial relations terms, than that between *regular* and *temporary* employees. *Seamen* and *public employees* of various categories are covered by different legislation. Here, in order to avoid any repetition of what has already been said in the Introduction, only the notion of and the legal nature of regular (permanent) employees and temporary employees, and the meaning of the *probationary* (*trial*) period for both kinds of employee, will be discussed. Also, the notion of *apprenticeship* means no more than that the Labour Standards Law lays down a few protective provisions concerning the exploitation of minor workers under the pretext of apprenticeship. The Labour Standards Law excludes from its coverage *domestic employees* in the home and *family workers* who work in plants employing only relatives actually living with the employer. Members of the employer's family who live outside his household, or those who work in plants employing other than family members, are covered by the Labour Standards Law. Thus, the most significant distinction in the legal sense is the distinction between employees employed for a definite term and those employed for an indefinite term.

§2. The Different Sorts of Individual Labour Contracts

82. The distinction between regular (permanent) and temporary employees does not necessarily coincide with the legal distinction between those employed for an indefinite term and those employed for a definite term. Since the notion of regular or permanent employees is not a legal but a practical one, the only legally meaningful distinction among Japanese workers is that between those employed for an indefinite and those employed for a definite term.

83. No legal formula is required for either kind of contract. Thus, it is often an important point – which requires careful examination – whether a certain contract was concluded for a definite or an indefinite term. Generally, however, the contract is interpreted as one for an indefinite term if no special mention has been made. The distinction between those for an indefinite term and those for a definite term is meaningful, as far as the law is concerned, only in connection with the termination of the contract. There are no distinctive legal provisions laid down for either group regarding working conditions, promotion, job assignment, the probationary period and so on. Thus, in principle, employers are free to employ a person for a definite term and to give them lower conditions (but not lower than the minimum standards stipulated by the Labour Standards Law) than those employed for an indefinite term. At the same time, employers are free to give favourable conditions to employees for an indefinite term and to deny such conditions to others who are also employed for an indefinite term. As a result, there are temporary employees employed for a definite term, and also some employed for an indefinite term, all of whom are denied the better working conditions recognised for the regular (permanent) employees.

I. The Individual Contract for an Indefinite Period

84. The parties to the contract concluded for an indefinite period are free to terminate the contract with notice. The period of notice is, for the employer, at least 30 days; and the employer may reduce this 30 days by paying an amount of money equivalent to the reduced days' average wage (Labour Standards Law, Art. 20). For employees, the period of notice is decided depending on the term of wage calculation, in accordance with civil law principles. So for those whose wage is calculated on a daily basis it is 14 days. For those whose wage is calculated for a certain period, notice should be given in the first half of the period and the contract terminated from the next period: for instance, monthly wage earners may terminate the contract from the next month if they give notice in the first half of the month. For those whose wage or salary is calculated for a period longer than six months the term of notice is three months (Civil Law, Art. 627). The Labour Standards Law protects employees by extending the period of notice for up to 30 days in the case of dismissal by the employer, regardless of the length of wage calculation. In the case of termination by the employee the civil law principles still apply. As far as both parties are concerned, notice is not necessary when there is a just cause for terminating the contract at once. However, with regard to *just cause*, the Labour Standards Law provides some protection for employees and certain principles have been developed through legal precedents in this connection (see below II and Part I, Chapter VI).

II. The Individual Contract for a Definite Period

85. The Contract for a definite period will finish automatically when the period expires, without any further action by the parties. During the period agreed upon the parties can terminate the contract when this is made necessary by an *inevitable reason*.[1] When the *inevitable reason* is the direct responsibility of one of the parties, the other party is entitled to compensation. The Labour Standards Law provides some protection for employees by amending the above civil law principle as follows:

(1) a contract for a definite period of more than one year is prohibited, except for those requiring a definite period for the completion of a project; and
(2) to end a contract for a definite period 30 days' notice is required, except for the following employees –
   (a) daily employed employees until they have been employed for longer than one month,
   (b) employees employed for a period not longer than two months,
   (c) employees employed for seasonal work lasting not longer than four months, and
   (d) employees on probation (trial).

When employees (a), (b) and (c) continue to be employed consecutively for longer than each specified period, the employer must give 30 days' notice to dismiss them. When employees (d) have been employed for more than 14 consecutive days the employer is also required to give 30 days' notice (Labour Standards Law, Art. 21). As a result of this protective legal provision, a contract for a definite term longer than each prescribed period for the respective types of employee is not to be treated as a contract for a definite period at least as far as the dismissal of employees is concerned. When an employee is still employed continuously after the prescribed period has expired, the same is true of his dismissal.

1. 'Inevitable reason' is regarded as being narrower than 'just cause' because termination of the contract for a definite period within the agreed period must be very extraordinary and more exceptional than that of the contract for an indefinite period. But, at the same time, it is broader than an 'act of God'.

§3. The Probation (Trial) Period

86. A probation (trial) period means a period specified by the contract, at the beginning of the employment contract, during which the employee's performance and ability is monitored and evaluated and during which either of the parties can terminate the contract as soon as they wish to do so. There is normally a tacit agreement that at the end of the period the employer will decide whether the employee is to be employed further or not. As we have already stated, the Labour Standards Law stipulates that after the first 14 days of the probation period the employer must give 30 days' notice to terminate the contract. Except for this legal requirement about the period of notice, the law says nothing about the probation period. Thus, several questions can be raised: are probation periods of 6 or 10 months legal as long as they are less than one year? Can probation periods be renewed or not? Opinions are divided. However, as we have mentioned, since after 14 days the employer should give 30 days' notice anyway, the major problem is really whether the employer can dismiss the employee more easily in terms of reasons than in the case of a normal employment contract. The case law has been imposing increasingly severe restrictions on the employer's greater freedom of dismissal during the probation period. Today, then, the Courts will permit only slightly more freedom of dismissal during the probation period; and therefore the above-mentioned questions are in fact theoretical rather than practical. The Courts will restrict the freedom of dismissal in cases where they find during any indication of abuse the longer or renewed probation period.

§4. Regulations concerning the Conclusion of Individual Contracts

87. An individual contract can only be concluded with the consent of both parties. Involuntary servitude is prohibited, except as a punishment for crime, by Art. 18 of the Constitution. This consent may be given tacitly, since the law does not require the written form for the conclusion of employment contracts. However, the Labour Standards Law requires the employer to clarify the wages, hours of work and other working conditions for the worker when they conclude the contract. If the real working conditions are different from those stated, the worker is entitled to cancel the contract and the employer must pay the travelling expenses incurred by the worker who has changed residence to take up the work if he returns home within 14 days of the cancellation.

88. In general, the nullity and cancellation of the contract because of threats, coercion, deceit, error or the incapacity of the parties is to be judged according to civil law principles. A contract which is contrary to imperative legal norms, public order or morality is also null and void. However, according to Art. 13 of the Labour Standards Law, when a contract provides for working conditions inferior to the standards set by the law only these conditions are invalid, and they are replaced by the conditions stipulated in the law. Article 16 of the Trade Union Law concerning contracts contrary to collective agreements and Art. 93 of the Labour Standards Law concerning contracts contrary to work rules have the same effect. Thus, the fact that the individual contract contradicts the provisions of the Labour Standards Law, collective agreements and work rules does not make the contract as a whole null and void, but only the provisions concerned; and the conditions otherwise stipulated take their place.

89. If a contract is null and void it is a principle of civil law that the invalidity or cancellation acts retroactively. But quite often labour relationship has in fact developed and progressed when the contract's nullity is declared or when it is cancelled. So legal precedents, taking notice of the actual relationship between employer and employee, have often recognised the existence of the contract in the past. For instance, in spite of the nullity of the contract, the employee's wage claim is admitted without trying to find the unnecessary legal detour of indemnity. Another typical case which shows respect for the facts rather than for the existence of a legal contractual relationship is the recognition of the employer's obligation to pay extra overtime rates for overtime work carried out illegally. Furthermore, generally speaking the contents of individual employment contracts are formulated by either collective agreements or work rules – with the contract itself becoming more and more a mere formality or a legal fiction, and the fact of actually providing labour becoming more important.

§5. Contractual Capacity and Restrictions on Employment

I. Minors

90. Minors under 20 years of age can only conclude any kind of contract with the permission of their parent or guardian; except for those contracts by which they merely receive certain rights or are exempted from certain obligations. This civil law principle is also applied to contracts of employment. However, the Labour Standards Law provides that the parent or guardian cannot conclude an employment contract in the place of the minor, and also that the minor has the right to receive wages independently and the parent or guardian may not receive the minor's wages by proxy. Concerning the employment of children under 15 years of age but over 12, work which does not harm their health or welfare, and which is not in manufacturing, mining, building, construction, transportation or other similar industries, is allowed outside school hours with the permission of the Labour Standards Office. Those less than 12 years old are only allowed to be employed in the theatre or in films, again with the permission of the Labour Standards Office. The employer must keep on the premises a census register which proves the age of all minors under 18, a teacher's certificate to prove that the employment is not hindering their education and a document giving the consent of their parents or guardians. The Labour Standards Law also provides extensive special protection for minors in respect of hours of work, night work and other working conditions (see Part I, Chapter IV).

II. Women

91. Both single and married women have the same capacity to conclude contracts of employment as men. Discrimination in working conditions because of sex is prohibited by the guarantee of equality of the sexes in Art. 14 of the Constitution. The Labour Standards Law in Art. 4 prohibits discrimination against women in the field of wages. On the other hand, the Labour Standards Law also provides rather extensive protection for women workers with regard to hours of work, night work and other working conditions. This causes real problems both in theory and in practice concerning the superficial contradiction between protection and equality (see Part I, Chapter IV).

III. Foreign Workers

92. Since the 2nd World War the Japanese Government has adopted a very restrictive policy towards the introduction of foreign workers into Japan; and this policy did not change during the period of serious labour shortage before the oil crisis. As a result of this policy there are no significant numbers of foreign workers in present-day Japan. Foreigners coming to Japan cannot get a visa with a work-permit on principle. One of the rare exceptions to this rule is when the worker's special abilities are irreplaceable and the Government grants him admission for this reason – for instance a Chinese cook who is needed by a Chinese restaurant. Another exception is the permission given to foreign workers to come to Japan for training. Since the number of such permitted workers in the labour force is very low, Japan is exceptional among the industrialised countries for having practically no problem with guest workers and for having kept the rather homogeneous quality of her own workers and avoided the trouble and unrest caused by guest workers both in industrial relations and in society in general. During the period of labour shortage the idea of introducing foreign labour was discussed, but because of the strict Government policy no serious attempt to do so was made.

Chapter II. Rights and Duties of the Parties in the Course of the Employment Relationship

93. In Japan, as in almost all other countries today, the rights and duties of employees and employers are not so much specified in individual labour contracts as formulated by rules established independently of mutual consent; namely, by collective agreements, work rules and numerous labour laws. Under the ever-increasing flow of labour legislation the employer is obliged to take quite a number of steps just in order to employ employees: such as obtaining various required documents and reporting, notifying or registering with Government offices details about conditions of work, accidents, the employment of certain categories of employees, social insurance, the introduction of certain machinery, equipment or facilities and so on. He must introduce measures to protect his employees' health and to ensure the safety of the plant. Employers are required to implement the steps necessary for the deduction and payment of the various contributions connected with the employment of workers – such as tax and social insurance fees – and also to pay part of these fees themselves. They must draw up work rules, display them to their employees and submit them to the Labour Standards Office if they employ more than 10 workers regularly. If his employees are organised, the employer is obliged to bargain with them if asked; and if an agreement is concluded as a result of this bargaining he should observe the obligations stipulated therein. When the employment contract ends, he has to provide a certificate giving details of the employment and pay all the funds and valuables due to the retired employee (including wages, reserves, bonds and savings). These obligations will be described in detail below. Here only the general principles of the rights and obligations, especially those stemming from the contract of employment but not explicitly mentioned either by the contract or the legislation, have been given.

§1. Employees' Duties

I. The Duty to Work

94. In the notion of 'subordinate labour', distinguished from 'independent work' as the fundamental factor in the employment relationship, there is an implicit acceptance of the fact that the employee has an obligation to do work under the command, authority and control of the employer and to obey his orders. This covers the duty of the employee to obey the provisions of the work rules and the orders of his superiors, and generally to do the work required of him during working time at the designated working place with the dedication expected of a 'normal' employee – that is, what can be expected of average workers, not of the best ones. How willing he should be to work on his own initiative without being specifically ordered to do so is a matter of loyalty, which is much emphasised in Japanese enterprises. However, legally speaking, such an expectation is a moral one and a matter of labour management. Those who are willingly co-operative will be promoted faster, but those who are not so keen will never be dismissed. Also, it is often pointed out as a very Japanese characteristic that Japanese employees are required to be devoted to the company's cause even outside working hours. The work rules of many enterprises stipulate that the employee must try to promote the company's good name and prestige, and avoid dishonouring it. However, legal precedents have been inclined to limit this broad obligation of loyalty and to restrict the employee's obligations mainly to matters concerning his job and within working hours. Some typical cases of this kind are those in which employees have been dismissed because they have committed a minor crime, such as violating the local regulations on outdoor assembly, indecency or obscenity, drunkenness, or even minor sneaking or embezzlement. The attitude of the Courts is usually to look first at the status of the employee and the nature of his job, and if he is not a very high ranking employee and his minor crime is unlikely to endanger the company's name, the Court will not find that such behaviour by an employee justifies his dismissal. On the other hand, if the crime is one which involves money – such as theft or embezzlement outside the company or work – the Courts will take it seriously if the employee concerned is doing a job which gives him easy access to the company's money.

95. The employee's obligation to work is understood to include an obligation to work in the place designated by the employer. In other words, the employer's right to transfer his employees has been regarded as part of his right to give orders. Especially in the case of regular employees, their frequent transfer from one job to another, and also from one work place to another, has been regarded as a matter of course connected with the life-time employment system. In this way the labour force is trained to meet the company's needs, and the employees can expect promotion by learning the different types of jobs which go on in their own enterprise. Thus, the labour force in general is not narrowly specialised in a particular job, but multi-skilled and experienced. The Japanese way of training on the job turned out to be more suitable for coping with rapid technological change; sustaining flexibility throughout the career of a worker by using him in various kind of jobs. Because employers and employees alike both expected the employee to be transferred around the several sections of the company throughout his life-time career, there were almost no cases of employees challenging the legal effect of the order to transfer until about 20 years ago. The only exceptions were cases in which employees claimed that the transfer was ordered because of their union activities (unfair labour practice cases). However, a growing number of transfers of a rather extreme nature were caused by the rapid technological change after 1960, and a changing attitude towards their work among young workers who have lost the traditional sense of loyalty and were more interested in their own family life and individual happiness, has led to an increasing number of cases concerning transfers being brought to the Courts and the Labour Relations Commissions. In some of these cases the transferred employees have argued that the transfer was ordered because of their union activities, their political thoughts or their sex. In other cases they have argued that the employers have abused their right to transfer by ordering a change of working place which was not really necessary; while, at the same time, the inconvenience caused to their lives and families by the transfer was very serious. The usual stand of the Courts and the Commissions on this issue is that in spite of the traditionally wide acceptance of the transfer in Japanese enterprises, there must be certain limits to the scope of possible transfers according to the job and status of the employee. For instance, in this context there are two types of employee in the larger firms: those employed at a particular plant who are expected to work only at that plant, and those employed at headquarters who are expected to work at every plant in the enterprise regardless of their job or whether they are white or blue collar. At the same time, despite rather flexible job assignments throughout their careers, there must be certain limits in terms of both parties' expectations. For instance, employees employed explicitly to do a special kind of job may not be transferred without their agreement. The employee who is employed as a radio or television announcer is not obliged to obey the order to work as a clerk or to do some other office job, and a cook in the company canteen cannot be transferred to a manual job in the factory. Within the scope of the accepted limits set by the nature of the employment contract, the employer should also pay attention to the problems likely to be caused by the transfer in the employee's private life. If the transfer is found to create grave difficulties for the employee, the Courts will look for the necessity or the inevitability of the transfer of the particular employee to the particular job. The Courts will declare the order to transfer null and void if they find that the transfer has caused serious difficulties for the employee, and that there was in fact a possibility of finding a substitute or that the transfer itself was not actually inevitable. The dismissal of an employee because he has disobeyed such an order will also be declared null and void, and the employee will be entitled to return to his former job or work place (see Part I, Chapter VI).

II. The Duty to Respect Professional Secrets

96. Given the traditional broad notion of employees' loyalty to the enterprise, ethically speaking the employee's obligation not to disclose his employer's trade secrets or confidential information is much emphasised. However, legally speaking the nature and extent of this obligation is not so clear. Generally, it is believed that an employee is free to use the skill and experience (or know-how) acquired through his employment to find another job after his contract has terminated. On the other hand, it is also generally accepted that he should not disclose the employer's secret documents and correspondence or abuse his connections with customers. Anyhow, such obligations rarely become legal issues; except in connection with the obligation to avoid competition after the termination of the contract (which will be discussed later, in Chapter VII), and in connection with the disclosure of company secrets or confidential information in order to protect the public interest.

97. The disclosure of information about the employer's activities is often regarded as a breach of the obligation of loyalty, rather than as a breach of the specific obligation to protect the employer's business secrets. In Japan, such matters are recognised as a matter of betrayal rather than as a breach of a specific legal obligation. Thus, whether the information disclosed is confidential and secret or not, is often rather irrelevant. The antagonistic attitude of the employee in attacking the company is the sole concern of the employer. Thus, when an employee attacks a company for causing pollution or for secretly supplying arms to the U.S. Forces, and does so as a form of political activity, the employer will dismiss him because of his antagonistic attitude towards the company rather than sue him for the damage caused by his act. Besides it being unpractical to seek reparation of damage from poor employees, the employer is always much more concerned with the company's name and discipline among the employees. However, the Courts usually apply a more business-like logic: looking for whether the employee's action was taken out of a genuine concern for the public interest; whether it caused serious harm to the company; whether the information disclosed was secret; and whether his attitude towards the company was contradictory with his obligations as a particular category of employee. The Courts often deny the employer's argument about the credibility of an employee who has challenged their company's good name, declaring that the employee's status was not high enough to endanger the company's honour.

§2. Employers' Duties

I. The Duty to Provide Work

98. It is not entirely self-evident that the employer has an obligation to provide work or to actually use the worker in addition to paying his wages. This question was first raised when an employer refused an employee access to the work place after his dismissal was declared null and void by the Court and while the employer was still paying his wages. The general tendency of the theories and the decided cases is to answer this question in the affirmative, although there is a minority body of opinion against it. The factors which should be taken into account are rather complex. Firstly, the employee's interest in the actual work should be admitted, since the work itself has a meaning in terms of his own personal dignity. And this should be recognised along with his interest in the wages. Secondly, especially if an unfair labour practice by the employer is involved, the employee's interest in having access to the work place is vital, because of the importance of union activity at the enterprise under the Japanese conditions of enterprise unionism. Thirdly, it is an established legal precedent that the Courts will order the employer to accept the right of the employee to work at his former work place if they find that his transfer was illegal.

II. The Provision of Decent Working Conditions

99. Article I, section I of the Labour Standards Law provides that working conditions must be such as will meet the needs of the worker who lives a life worthy of a human being. From this and other provisions which aim to secure the decent and humane treatment of workers, one can conclude that there is an obligation on employers to have proper concern for the welfare of their employees. This obligation requires them not only to observe the various protective labour law provisions governing safety, hygiene and other working conditions, but also to endeavour to promote the raising of standards above the minimum laid down by the legislation (Art. 1, sect. 2 of the Labour Standards Law). The extensive nature of this obligation is exemplified by the provisions in the Labour Standards Law which require the employer to pay the transport costs not only of female employees and employees less than 18 years old who have been dismissed and who are going back home within 14 days, but also of those who have terminated their contracts because they have found the actual conditions to be different from what was stated before the contracts were concluded. The employer also has an obligation to allow his employees the necessary time-off to exercise their right to vote and other civil rights, and to carry out their public duties.

III. The Establishment of Work Rules, etc.

100. As well as having to inform prospective employees about the conditions of work before concluding contracts with them, the employer who employs more than ten employees continuously must also draw up his work rules and submit them to the Labour Standards Office. He must ask for the opinion of the majority union, or for the opinion of the representative of the majority of employees in the absence of a majority union in the enterprise, before drawing up the work rules. The following working conditions must always be laid down in the work rules:

1. hours of work, rest hours, holidays, vacations and shifts;
2. wages – methods of deciding, computation and date of payment, promotion and so on;
3. matters concerning retirement and dismissal.

If there are any of the following benefits, systems or measures the employer must also stipulate them in the work rules:

1. retirement allowances, bonuses, minimum wage and so on;
2. the cost charged to the employees for food, equipment and other expenses;
3. regulations covering safety, sanitation and related matters;
4. regulations about vocational training;
5. regulations governing accident compensation and relief for injury and illness sustained outside work;
6. official commendations or sanctions (disciplinary measures);
7. other stipulations applicable to all employees.

The employer has to inform his employees of the work rules and also of the gist of the Labour Standards Law and its by-laws by displaying or posting them in places accessible to all employees.

IV. The Employer's Obligations at the End of the Labour Contract

101. The employer must provide the retiring or dismissed worker, on his request, with a certificate giving details of the period of employment, the type of work done, his position in the enterprise, and his wages. He may not insert in the certificate anything which the employee does not ask for. Also, he must not conspire to send or circulate information about the nationality, creed, social status or union activities of the employee, nor make any secret mark on the certificate. Furthermore, again on request, he must pay all wages and return any reserves, bonds, savings or other funds and valuables belonging to the employee within 7 days of his retirement, death or dismissal.

Chapter III. Hours of Work, Overtime and Holidays

§1. Hours of Work

102. Hours of work means the actual working time excluding rest hours and summing up, regardless of a change of work place. There are no legal provisions about how working time should in fact be calculated; so does it start when the employees enter the gate and continue until they leave, or does it start only when they make themselves ready to begin work and end when they finish working? The Labour Standards Law only stipulates that for underground work the hours of work include the whole period from pit-head to pit-head, including recesses. Thus, for ordinary work this will be a matter to be decided by agreement or in the work rules. In the absence of any stipulation or established practice, the Courts have laid down that it should be calculated from gate to gate. However, even if, for example, it is laid down in the work rules that working time starts from the time when the employees get ready to begin work and ends when they actually finish work, the question is still likely to arise as to whether the time needed to get ready for work and to finish work – changing clothes, washing and so on – should be included in the working time or not. As for those employees who work outside the premises and take their work home without coming back, and those who are on business trips, it is presumed that they are keeping normal working hours unless they are ordered to do otherwise or have proof of having worked extra hours.

103. The maximum normal working hours for adult male employees are 8 hours per day and 48 hours per week, with the following rather extensive exceptions which allow the employer to extend working hours beyond these limits.

1. In agriculture, forestry, animal husbandry and fishing.
2. Employees in a supervisory or management post, or who are employed in a confidential capacity.
3. Employees engaged in watching and intermittent labour with the approval of the Labour Standards Office.
4. The hours of work in each day or each week may be extended, as long as the average hours over 4 weeks do not exceed 48 hours and this is stipulated in the work rules or other rules beforehand (uneven distribution of working hours).
5. In the case of an accident or some other unavoidable temporary situation, with the permission of the Labour Standards Office.
6. In Government and other public offices when there is a temporary need.
7. Work essential for the public convenience or required to meet other special needs specified by an ordinance of the Labour Ministry – in such industries as transportation, freight, sales, banking, insurance, entertainment, post and telecommunications, education, research, medical services, hotels, restaurants, snack-bars, recreation services, incineration, cleaning, butchery and Government offices.

104. The employer should provide rest hours totalling at least forty-five minutes for more than 6 hours' work and at least one hour for more than 8 hours' work. Rest hours should be given to all employees at the same time, except if the employer has received permission from the Labour Standards Office to do otherwise. The employer must not interefere with the use made by his employees of their rest hours. Exceptions (1), (2), (3) and (7) in the paragraph above concerning working hours are also permitted in the case of rest hours.

§2. Holidays

105. The employer must provide his employees with at least one rest day per week. Exceptions (1), (2), (3), (5) and (6) described above concerning working hours are also permitted in connection with work on holidays. National holidays, which amount to 12 days per year, are not legally binding in the private sector but today most offices and factories do give them. Also, the 5 day working week is becoming gradually more popular in the private sector, but still is confined to the larger enterprises since the minimum legal requirement is 6 working days. Government offices are still open on Saturdays, but by dividing the employees into two groups a system giving employees a five day week every other week is operated in most of them. The actual total working hours in Japan are much longer than most Western industrialised countries (see Table XV) because of limited acceptance of the 5 day week, the general practice of longer overtime and a low consumption rate of annual vacation as described below.

Table XV

International Comparison of Actual Working Hours per Year
(production workers in manufacturing industry)

Year	Japan	US	England	W. Germany	France
1975	2,043	1,888	1,678	1,923	1,830
1980	2,162	1,893	1,728	1,887	1,782
1981	2,146	1,898	1,707	1,891	1,769
1982	2,136	1,851	1,690	1,891	1,733

Source: Japan: Labour Ministry, Monthly Labour Statistics, ILO, Yearbook of Labour Statistics and EC, Labour Costs in Industry, 1975.

§3. Overtime

106. Overtime means work done outside normal working hours and on holidays. Overtime is allowed in the case of exception (5) above, and also when the employer concludes an agreement with the majority union, or the representative of the majority of the employees in the absence of a majority union, and submits the written agreement to the Labour Standards Office. For adult male workers there is no legal limit to the amount of overtime they can do. The only limits are those imposed by the Labour Standards Law for underground work and other work specified as injurious to health by an ordinance of the Labour Ministry. In these jobs the maximum overtime allowed is 2 hours per day. The employer must pay wages for overtime at an increased rate of at least 25 per cent above normal wages. The legal approach to overtime has been criticised on the grounds that employees may well be willing to work for longer if they are guaranteed higher wages, and so the employers will have no trouble getting their agreement. This means that there is really no limitation on the length of overtime, except for underground and other specified types of work. This is one of the reasons for longer working hours in Japan today.

§4. Night Work

107. Night work is defined by the Labour Standards Law as that work done between 10 p.m. and 5 a.m., and it can be changed to that done between 11 p.m. and 6 a.m. by the Ministry of Labour if it proves necessary in a particular area or season. For the adult male worker the only regulation about night work is that payment for it must be at the increased rate of at least 25 per cent above normal wages. For women and minors there are special regulations concerning hours of work in general which will be described in the next Chapter.

§5. Annual Vacations

108. The minimum length of annual paid vacation is 6 days for those who have been employed continuously for one year and who were present for over eighty per cent of the total working days in this year. The number of vacation days is increased by one day for each year of length of service up to 20 days. During the vacation the employer should pay the employee his average or normal wages. The employee may take his vacation 'consecutively or separately' whenever he likes during the year; but the employer may change the date of the employee's vacation if it disturbs the normal operation of the enterprise. The word 'separately' was added to the original draft during the process of enacting the law. The reason for this amendment to the original draft is the absence of the annual vacation as a custom in Japan. As a result of this legislative wording, and also because of the unfamiliar nature of the annual vacation, the way of using the annual vacation has taken a rather peculiar form.

109. The overwhelming majority of vacation days are used for various private matters such as shopping, going to the city or the municipal offices, visiting the children's school, going to the home country and so on; or else when the employee does not feel like working or is a little unwell. They are mostly taken one or two days at a time. Vacations for a long time like a week or two are quite a recent phenomenon in Japanese society, and so often some of the vacation days to which employees are entitled are left unused at the end of the year (42 per cent of total entitled vacations were not used in 1982) and are paid-off by the employer – although in fact such paying-off is deemed to be illegal.

Chapter IV. The Protection of Women and Minors

§1. The Protection of Women Workers in General

110. Women workers are allowed to do overtime amounting to 2 hours a day, 6 hours a week or 150 hours a year. However, female employees engaged in accountancy may work more than 6 hours' overtime in a week provided they do not do more than 12 hours in 2 weeks. Women are not allowed to work at night, underground or on the weekly holiday. Exceptionally, in an emergency, they may do extra overtime or holiday work; and it is also generally permitted in agriculture, animal husbandry, medical and service industries, the telephone service and the other jobs specified by an ordinance of the Labour Ministry as harmless to the health and welfare of women. This exception does not, however, apply to women workers under 18 years of age in service industries. Dangerous jobs and jobs which involve the carrying of heavy weights, as specified by an ordinance of the Labour Ministry, are prohibited for women.

§2. Maternity Protection

111. Maternity leave of six weeks before and after childbirth is guaranteed. The woman does not have to take the leave before the birth if she does not need it, but afterwards she must take a minimum of five weeks' leave regardless of her wishes. A woman nursing a baby less than one year old is entitled to take at least 30 minutes' nursing time twice a day during working hours. The employer should provide leave of absence, upon request, for a woman who suffers badly from menstruation or who is doing a job specified by an ordinance of the Labour Ministry as harmful to menstruation.

§3. Discrimination and Equality

112. The Labour Standards Law lays down the principle of equal pay for equal work between the sexes (Art. 4). With regard to working conditions other than wages, Art. 3 of the same law, however, prohibits discrimination by reason of nationality, creed or social status, but not sex. The omission of sexual equality from Art. 3 is explained by the fact that the law, in providing special protection for women, actually presumes the unequal treatment of the sexes. It has been argued from another perspective that equal treatment with regard to working conditions other than wages is in fact taken for granted and actually implied by Arts. 3 and 4. Article 14 of the Constitution prohibits discrimination because of race, creed, social status, family origin or sex. It may be said that the protection provided for women does not contradict a policy of sexual equality since women are handicapped by their physical characteristics. A number of legal precedents have established the illegality of an earlier retirement age for women and retirement on marriage using this argument.

113. The Labour Ministry's Study Committee on Labour Standards issued a report in 1978 suggesting the abolition of some of the protective provisions of the Labour Standards Law and the introduction of legislation to guarantee equal opportunity for women in employment. But public opinion has been sharply divided on these issues and sex discrimination is likely to remain the most significant type of discrimination in Japan. Interest in equality in employment, working conditions and promotion for women has grown as women enter the work force in higher numbers and have started to remain in employment after marriage and childbirth. The number of female employees almost doubled between 1970 and 1982 (nearly 35 per cent of the total number of employees). The average age of female workers rose during the same period from 26 years to 35 years. In 1982, more than half of the women employed outside the home were over 35, up from 39 per cent in 1970. The percentage of married female workers also increased from 44.7 per cent in 1962 to 68.5 per cent in 1982 and the average length of service of women workers rose from four years in 1970 to 6.3 years in 1982.

114. More and more women have been entering the workforce in recent years, yet many companies will employ women only in temporary, part-time or low-paying jobs. Job segregation by sex is common. Most employers will not hire women university graduates: only 27 per cent of companies that recruited university graduates offered employment to female graduates, according to the Labour Ministry's Survey on Personnel Management of Women Workers in 1981. Similarly, discrimination in retirement policies, promotion and training opportunities helps keep women out of higher paying jobs. While the Labour Ministry has issued guidelines for the abolition of a lower retirement age for women with some success, the Ministry's survey showed that fewer than 40 per cent of companies employ women in positions above the level of supervisor and 20 per cent of these companies provide no training whatsoever for women workers. Forty per cent provide different kinds of training for women and men. In spite of the legal principle of equal pay for equal work, in 1982, the average wage for women workers was 52.8 per cent of that of men.

115. Other types of discrimination are less pervasive, for a variety of reasons. Religious discrimination has never been a political concern, perhaps because the Japanese people are rather indifferent and tolerant of different religious creeds. Age, sexual preference and marital status also have not been raised extensively as bases for discrimination. Political opinion has at times been an issue in internal union affairs as well as employment dismissals. The courts have usually found dismissals on this basis to be illegal. Few legal cases have involved discrimination based on race, colour or ethnicity, simply because the population is fairly monolithic and homogenous, although this does not mean such discrimination does not exist. Discrimination because of race and nationality may present a greater problem in the future because of the expected growth in the number of foreign workers due to the increasing internationalisation of the Japanese economy.

116. For these reasons, most court activity has been in the area of sex discrimination. Courts have held that dismissal because of marriage, pregnancy and childbirth is contrary to Art. 14 of the Constitution. There have been few cases, however, that challenge discrimination in promotion or wages and none in refusal of employment to serve as precedent. The Courts traditionally have respected employers' freedom to hire and women have been reluctant to use the courts to change discriminatory employment policies such as job segregation. (Expected new legislation may provide the Labour Ministry with the authority to issue administrative guidance to correct sex segregation in employment.) The courts place the burden of proof on the plaintiff who challenges the legality of discriminatory action. However, the courts often switch burden to the defendant when the plaintiff has reasonably convinced the court of the probability of discrimination. Nonetheless, sex discrimination remains difficult to prove in the Japanese courts. The courts are also limited in the types of remedies they may order: the courts may declare a discriminatory dismissal null and void and in effect provide for reinstatement; a plaintiff in a refusal to hire case may recover damages, but there is no precedent for the issuance of affirmative orders. Despite these limitations, the courts remain virtually the only enforcement agency in Japan against discrimination.

§4. The Protection of Minors

117. The prohibitions and restrictions on the employment of workers less than 18 years old have already been described above in Chapter I, §4. The exceptions to the principle of the 8 hour working day and 48 hour working week permitted for adult workers (such as the uneven distribution of working hours, longer working hours in certain industries or jobs and overtime work) are not allowed for minors under 18 years old. For those under 15 years old who are only permitted to work in specified industries the maximum is 7 hours a day, 42 hours a week (including school hours). For those more than 15 years old, but less than 18 years old, working time may be extended to 10 hours a day when the hours of work on one day a week are reduced to 4 and the total for the week does not exceed 48. Overtime, holiday work and underground work are prohibited for minors under 18 years old. Night work is also prohibited, except for those over 16 years of age who are working on shifts. Exceptions to the prohibition of night work and work on the weekly holidays are allowed in agriculture, animal husbandry, medical services and the telephone service. Minors under 18 years of age are also prohibited from working in the dangerous and harmful jobs specified by an ordinance of the Labour Ministry.

Chapter V. Remuneration and Benefits

§1. Pay Systems

118. It is generally accepted that the Japanese wage system, including retirement allowances, is highly dependent on age and length of service rather than on skill or job evaluation. Although recently the trend has been to emphasise evaluation more than in the past, and although some research done by economists suggests that the correlation between the amount of wages, the length of service and age is not as different from that in Western countries as was expected, the differrence still exists both in statistical fact and, more especially, in attitudes and ideas. As Tables XVI and XVII show, the differences in wages by age and length of service are greater in Japan than in the major European countries. Even more important is the fact that in Japan, wage calculations are based on education and length of service. Starting wages are decided according to the employee's level of education rather than his ability, and then basic wages are increased annually according to his length of service. Only after several years of service do differences caused by promotion gradually appear which are based on the individual's merit. However, this does not deny the basic pattern of an annual wage increment automatically connected with the length of service and allowing little scope for divergence from the norm. The usual pattern of Japanese wages is illustrated very roughly in Figure III.

Table XVI

Wage Differences by Length of Service of Male Production Workers
(100=wages for less than 2 years length of service)

Years of service	less than 2	3–4	5–9	10–19	20–more
Japan (1982)	100	112.7	126.2	149.4	175.3
West Germany (1972)	100	106.9	111.8	113.8	112.8
France (1972)	100	111.5	119.9	128.7	130.9
Italy (1972)	100	106.3	112.1	123.1	128.2

Source: Labour Ministry, Basic Statistics of Wage Structure, 1982 for Japan and EC, *Structure of Earnings in Industry*, 1972 for other countries.

119. Another characteristic of the Japanese wage system is that the basic wage includes various types of allowances such as family, commuting, housing and regional allowances, allowances for foremen, supervisors and other positions, for special jobs, special work, technical work, high attendance rates and subsidised living expenses – not to mention the other allowances for merit and piecework or payment by results. Bonuses, which in most cases are paid

TABLE XVII

Wage Differences by Age of Male Production Workers

(100 = wages for 21–24 year old)

	younger than 18 year old	18–20	21–24	25–29	30–34	35–39	40–44	45–49	50–54	55–59	older than 60	total
Japan 1982	63.8	84.0	100.0	123.8	145.4	162.0	167.0	166.7	162.1	141.2	105.4	143.4
US 1969	–	–	100.0	124.1		122.6		122.6		115.6		118.1
England 1982	54.4	79.2	100.0	108.6	115.8		115.4		109.4		101.7	107.1
West Germany 1972	58.8	88.1	100.0	105.5	108.0	108.2	106.9	105.4	103.0	99.8	95.9	103.5
France 1972	70.5	87.2	100.0	108.8	113.0	113.9	113.4	111.6	109.9	106.6	102.5	106.1
Italy 1972	70.5	88.6	100.0	108.5	111.7	112.7	111.6	111.0	110.2	109.3	101.2	108.5

Monthly regular payment of manufacturing industry for Japan.
Weekly net earnings of all industry for US.
Hourly net earnings of all for other countries.
18–20 means 18–19 for Japan and 21–24 means 20–24 for Japan and the US.
Source: Ministry of Labour, *Basic Statistics of Wage Structure*, 1982 for Japan, Dept. of Commerce, *Current Population Survey* for the US, Ministry of Employment, *New Earnings Survey*, 1982 for England and EC, *Structure of Earnings in Industry* for other countries.

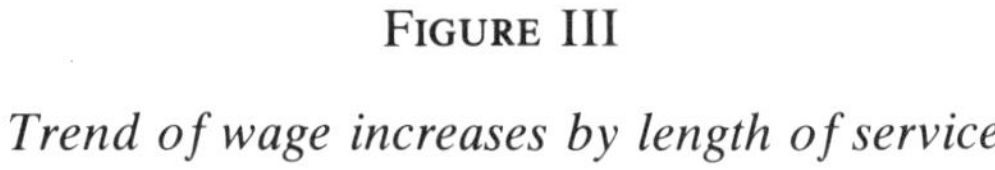

FIGURE III

Trend of wage increases by length of service

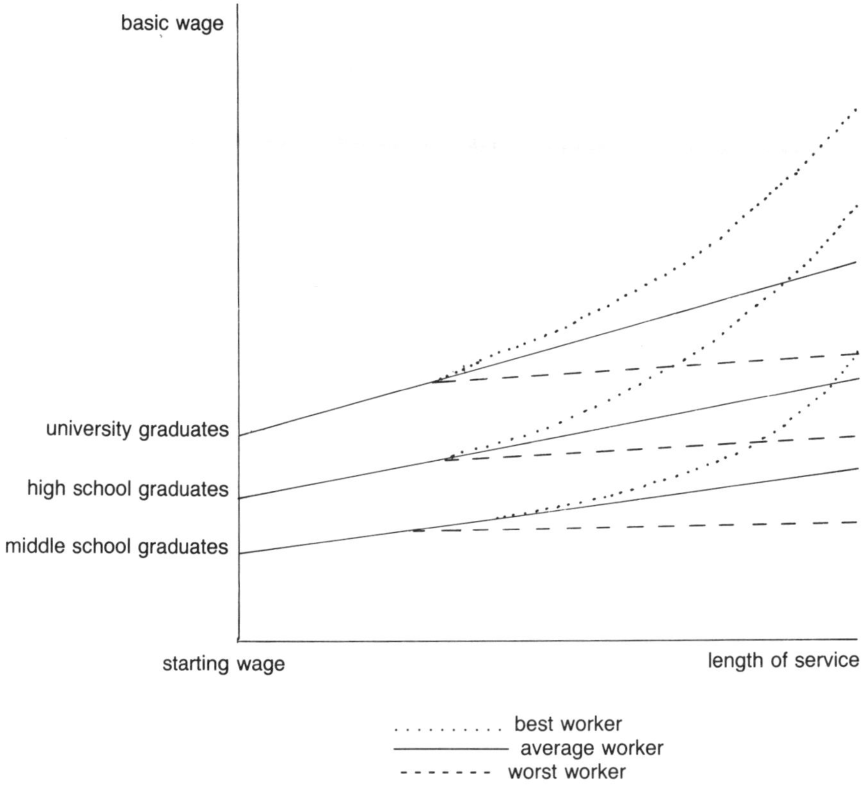

twice a year at the end of the year and in the summer, are a very important part of wages; being equivalent to about 5 months' wages in total for a year on average, and often amounting to more than 6 months' wages. As we have already mentioned, retirement allowances paid in lump sums and often accompanied by pensions are also regarded as a part of wages; and a very important part too, which may mean more than 25 months' wages for those retiring after 30 years of service. And the total amount of pension to be paid on top of the lump sum payment, which is what happens in nearly 20 per cent of all enterprises and more than half of the larger enterprises, is about equal to the amount of the lump sum payment.

120. As a result of having a wage system essentially based on length of service and education, the wage differentials caused by the factors which we have already mentioned (such as age and length of service) have been rather conspicuous. In addition to this, because wage determination (including bargaining) is done mainly at enterprise level, the differentials caused by differences in the size of enterprises and regional differences have been important. Other differentials, between regular and temporary workers or between workers of different status and sex, have also been characteristic of the wage structure in Japan. Today, although these differentials do still exist, they have become narrower in every respect since the serious labour shortage before the oil crisis.

§2. The Notion of Wages

121. Wages are defined by the Labour Standards Law as including all the payments made by the employer to the employee as remuneration for work, whether they are called wages, salaries, allowances, bonuses or whatever (Art. 11). Although the Law prohibits the employer from paying wages other than in cash as a principle, it is in fact allowed if otherwise provided for by law, order or agreement. Thus, the problem arises as to what extent goods and other benefits given to the employee by the employer should be regarded as a part of wages. Generally, such goods and benefits are regarded as a part of wages:

1. when they are provided in the place of wages in cash, usually accompanied by the deduction of the equivalent amount from the wages; and
2. when their provision is agreed in the contract as an addition to wages in cash.

However, they are not regarded as a part of wages if the employees pay a price or fee for them, or if they form a part of the welfare facilities of the enterprise. Some payments in cash, such as the money given by the enterprise to the employee on marriage, for the funeral of a member of his family or for a personal accident or casualty, are not regarded as a part of wages as long as the precise, detailed conditions of the payments are not laid down in the work rules or agreements. The concrete application of the principles raises some difficult questions, of which the following are examples. The tips earned by waiters and waitresses are not wages unless there is an arrangement by which the employer takes all the tips received from customers and divides them between the employees. Housing provided by the employer is regarded as a part of wages only when the employer pays a housing allowance of equal value to those not living in company accommodation.

122. Although in principle wages are remuneration for the work done by the employee, in practice they are now quite often paid for periods during which no work is done at all. Such remuneration includes payments to replace notice of dismissal, the payment of wages during the annual vacation, during time-off caused by an accident at work and so on. The Labour Standards Law provides a rather detailed definition of the 'average wage' in Art. 12. According to this provision, the 'average wage' means the quotient obtained by dividing the total amount of wages for a period of three months (or the period of employment if this is less than 3 months) preceding the day on which the calculation of the average wage became necessary or the final day of the wage calculation period if it exists) by the number of days in this period; but the amount shall not be less than the amount computed by one of the following methods:

1. If the wages are calculated by the working day or the working hour, or paid at piece-rates or by result, 60 per cent of the quotient obtained by dividing the total sum of the wages by the number of working days during that period;
2. If a part of the wage is defined by the month, week or any other fixed period, an aggregate of the quotient obtained by dividing the total sum of these parts by the number of days during that period and the sum calculated by the foregoing method.

If the above-mentioned period includes any of the following periods, the days and wages in these periods shall be excluded from the days and total amount of wages:

1. rest days for medical treatment necessitated by an accident at work;
2. rest days before and after childbirth guaranteed by the law;
3. rest days necessitated by something for which the employer is responsible;
4. the probation period.

The amount of wages on which the 'average wage' is calculated does not include extraordinary wages and those paid periodically at more than three month intervals. Concerning the inclusion of payments other than in money, the Labour Minister provides detailed standards. The amount of 'average wages' for the daily worker is also defined by the Labour Minister.

§3. Regulations concerning the Payment of Wages

123. Wages must be paid in cash and in full directly to the workers themselves. They must be paid at least once a month on a definite date, except for extraordinary wages, bonuses and the like specified by an ordinance of the Labour Ministry. Payment other than in cash may be permitted if otherwise provided for by law, order or labour agreement. Deductions from the wages may also be permitted if otherwise provided for by law, order or a written agreement with the majority union or, if there is no majority union, with the representative of the majority of employees. However, even if such agreement exists, deductions to offset the employer's claim against an employee are only permissible within the limit of one fourth of the total amount of wages in a payment period.

124. Exceptions to the above-mentioned standards which are in common use are the deduction of tax, social security fees, union dues and fees under the check-off system; the repayment of debts to the employer; the payment of fees and payment for benefits and goods provided by the employer under an agreement to this effect. However, the employer may not make a contract fixing in advance either the sum payable for breach of contract or the amount of indemnity for damage caused by the employee's negligence; and neither may he deduct the money advanced or make any other claim on the condition to work (prohibition of compulsory labour by advance payment). Concerning payment in cash, payment by cheque and payment into the employee's bank account have recently become controversial issues. The latter is admitted on condition that the payment is made into an account designated by the employee and that the total amount of wages can be withdrawn on pay-day. But the former tends to be denied, at least legally, which perhaps reflects the unpopularity of the use of the cheque in Japan. The deduction of the amount of overpayment of wages is regarded as lawful even without agreement since it is only a matter of settlement or adjustment. On the other hand, some difficult legal problems arise in this connection with regard to wages during strikes which will be described later (see Part II, Chapter V).

125. When an employee requires money for an emergency use such as childbirth, disease, accident or something else specified by an ordinance of the Labour Ministry, the employer shall pay the accrued wages before pay-day (emergency payment).

§4. Guarantee of the Payment of Wages on the Employer's Insolvency

126. The wage claims of employees are protected by the already-described regulations on the payment of wages: in cash, in full and by direct and periodical payment. Thus, the delayed payment of wages can be punished by a fine. But of course it is possible that the enterprise may go bankrupt, so leaving delayed wages unpaid. The civil law gives priority to wage claims for the last three months against other claims. However, in actuality there are quite often other claims on the enterprise, especially large ones secured by bonds and mortgages, and as a result the priority given to wages does not really mean much. The Law Concerning the Security of Wage Payment etc. of 1976 introduced special measures under which the Government must pay the unpaid wages in the place of the employer who has become unable to pay owing to serious financial difficulties or even bankruptcy.

§5. The Minimum Wage

127. The employer must guarantee a fixed wage proportionate to the working hours of those workers who are paid piece-rates or by results. This minimum fixed wage is interpreted as guaranteeing a certain amount of income to the employee, but the minimum amount is not specified in the law. The Labour Ministry says that the size of the fixed wage should be defined so as to guarantee an amount which is not drastically lower than normal income.

128. So far in Japan there is no fixed flat-rate minimum wage applied to all industries at a national level. The Minimum Wage Law of 1959 prescribes two kinds of minimum wage. The first is that decided by the Labour Minister or the

Chief of the Prefectural Labour Standards Bureau upon the request (based on agreement) of all the employers and unions covered by a collective agreement or agreements with substantially the same provisions regarding minimum wages, and applied to the majority of workers of the same kind and their employers in a certain district. The second is that decided by the Labour Minister or the Chief of the Prefectural Labour Standards Bureau on the basis of the research and deliberations of the Minimum Wage Deliberation Commission, and applied to certain industries, jobs or districts. In deciding on the former type the Minister or the Chief should also ask the opinion of the Minimum Wage Deliberation Commission. The Commission is set up both at national level (Central M.W.D.C.) and at local level (Local M.W.D.C.), and is composed of three delegations: workers, employers and the public. As yet minimum wages have mainly been decided for the traditionally low wage industries. In 1982 the national minimum wage was ¥5,296 per day for mining and ¥3,300–3,600 for other industries. The average amount of the industrial minimum wage was ¥3,515 and that of the regional one is ¥3,516.

§6. Wage Levels

129. The international comparison of wage levels is a very tricky business if we consider the varying exchange rate and the difficulty of comparing the prices of consumer goods in different countries. Tables XVIII and XIX give an idea of Japanese wage levels which should be taken as an illustration of many possible figures. According to these statistics we could say that the Japanese wage level is nominally about 60 per cent of the US level, slightly lower than the German and English, and higher than the French and Italian levels. It is estimated much lower in real rates than those of the US and Germany. However, such estimations of real wage rates could be subject to a lot of argument. And furthermore in order to estimate the actual living standards of the workers we need take several other factors into consideration – such as non-monetary fringe benefits, company welfare and social welfare costs, not to mention various cultural factors including the environment. Really the only thing we can say here is that it is hardly plausible to argue that Japan is still taking advantage of lower wage levels.

§7. Equal Pay

130. The principle of equal pay for equal work is promulgated by the Labour Standards Law only in connection with men and women, as we have already seen. With wage differences by education, length of service, age, size of enterprise, region and industry prevailing, and wage negotiation and determination taking place at enterprise level, the principle of equal pay for equal work is hardly acceptable except in ideology. Of course the idea has been advocated most enthusiastically by the younger workers who are becoming more and more aware of the value of their flexibility and efficiency in a time of

TABLE XVIII

International Comparison of Nominal Wages (Manufacturing Production Workers) 1982

	Period of Wage Calculation	Size of Wage (Yen)	Rate (Japan=100)
Japan	Month	233,632	
	Week	53,915	100
	Hour	1,322	
USA	Hour	2,117	160
UK	Hour	1,394	105
W. Germany	Hour	1,503	114
France	Hour	1,127	85
Italy	Hour	(1,114)	(88)
Canada	Hour	2,069	156.5
Sweden	Hour	1,549	117
Norway	Hour	1,920	145
Australia	Hour	(1,216)	(96)
Mexico	Month	(108,006)	(48)
Korea	Month	70,478	30

Source: Japanese Productivity Centre. *Practical Labour Statistics* (Tokyo: 1984).
( )=1981 figures.

TABLE XIX

International Comparison of Real Wages (Manufacturing Production Workers) (Japan = 100)

	Hourly Wage		Nominal Rate		Real Rate	
Countries	1978	1979	1978	1979	1978	1979
Japan	981.3	1,025.1 yen	100	100	100	100
USA	6.75	7.32 dollar	144.8	156.6	205.2	197.9
W. Germany	14.91	15.71 DM	159.2	183.3	174.3	175.3

Source: Japanese Productivity Centre, *Practical Labour Statistics* (Tokyo: 1981). Calculation by the Labour Ministry.

rapid technological development. This trend has certainly contributed to the narrowing of the wage differential over several years; as has the growing difficulty of recruiting young, competent workers. Although the time of great labour shortage is over, the shortage of younger workers is expected to continue, taking into account the prospect of further technological development in the future and the trend towards attaining an increasingly higher level of education among the coming younger generations. Also, Japanese society is having to face the problem of older workers whose ability is destined to lose its value given technological development, and whose number is growing because of increased life expectancy. The high cost of these older workers, resulting from the seniority wage system, is now imposing a heavy burden on Japanese enterprises. Thus, the trend towards equal pay will be even more pronounced in the future.

§8. Remuneration during Time-Off

I. Rest-Day Allowances

131. If the employer is responsible for causing the rest day he shall pay an allowance equivalent to at least 60 per cent of the average wage. This rest-day allowance provided for by Art. 26 of the Labour Standards Law is compulsory in the sense that it is enforced by the threat of a fine. Theoretically, the employer is liable to pay the full wage if work became impossible because of his negligence or intention. Thus the purpose of the rest-day allowance is to guarantee 60 per cent of the average wage as a minimum, and employees can still claim the rest of their wages using ordinary civil law procedure. Also, the legal precedents have tended to interpret the employer's liability to pay rest-day allowances more broadly than the civil law. For instance, closure because of financial difficulties, a lack of materials caused by a strike held by another union and a strike in the supplying company are a few examples of cases in which it was held that the employer should pay rest-day allowances. During an illegal lock-out the employer must pay the rest-day allowance quite apart from his liability to pay the full wages (see Part II, Chapter V). Of course in all these cases, if the employer has paid a rest-day allowance and then been found liable in civil law to pay the full wages, he is only obliged to pay the difference between the full wages and the amount already paid in rest-day allowances.

II. Accidents at Work and Occupational Diseases

132. During a period of incapacity for work caused by an accident at work or occupational disease the employer must pay the employee 60 per cent of the average wage as 'non-work compensation'. Failure to pay this allowance brings the threat of punishment by imprisonment or fine; although in fact it is actually paid as a benefit under the Workmen's Compensation Insurance Act of 1947 which covers all employees. If the employer is found to be liable for the accident under the civil law, the employee is entitled to claim the difference between his full wages and the amount of compensation.

III. Leave of Absence

133. The only leave of absence to which the employee is legally entitled (besides the already-mentioned leave for childbirth and menstruation, and the annual holiday) is time-off work to carry out official duties. The employer must give the employee leave of absence during working hours to exercise his franchise and other civil rights and to execute his public duties. This time-off is not necessarily with pay, but wages are sometimes paid depending on the length of the absence. For instance, a short absence from work in order to vote is permitted without a wage-cut, while a longer leave of absence (necessitated by election to public office or even to the legislature) will be without pay. In most enterprises the latter situation will be treated as a reason for suspension (see the next Chapter).

134. Most companies provide various kinds of leave of absence: sick leave, leave for marriage, for the funeral of a family member, for union actitivies and for other reasons with the permission of the management. Sick leave of a few days is allowed without a doctor's certificate. The right to short periods of leave to undertake union activities may be provided for by collective agreement. Longer leave for full-time union officials is treated as a reason for suspension. Such leave is only given without pay, as otherwise it would be regarded as giving financial assistance to the union fund and this is prohibited as an unfair labour practice (see Part II, Chapter VI). Other leaves of absence – including those guaranteed by law – can be given with or without pay depending on the agreement, or often on the provisions of the work rules. In many enterprises wages are not deducted for a short period of illness, especially in the case of a monthly paid employee. During sick leave and maternity leave employees receive approximately 60 per cent of their average wages from the Health Insurance scheme which covers all employees.

§9. The Suspension Period

135. The notion of suspending the employment contract is not very widespread in Japanese industrial relations. Instead, most enterprises have a system called the 'suspension period', during which the contract continues to be in force except for work and wage payment. The 'suspension period' is a period during which the employee is released from the obligation to work and wages are not paid or only partly paid. Thus, the difference between this period and the leave of absence is not very clear; except that they are stipulated in a different way and 'suspension' is usually for a longer period.

136. There are two kinds of suspension period. One is a period of incapacity for work which the employer tolerates without dismissing the employee. Such a period may be when the employee is seriously ill, when he becomes a union official, or when he undertakes full-time training or study (even abroad). Wages are sometimes paid in full, sometimes in part and sometimes not at all;

depending on the reason and the length of the period. For instance, if the employee is ill he gets 80 per cent of his wages for the first six months, 60 per cent for the next six months and so on. The maximum period tolerated is also different – depending on the reason – but it can be as much as two or three years. Legal problems may arise as to whether the employment contract then ends altogether or revives fully. It depends both on the reason for the suspension and the situation at the end of the period. If the incapacity for work still exists the employer is entitled to dismiss the employee; otherwise the employee is entitled to resume his full employee status.

137. The other kind of suspension period is suspension as a punishment or suspension while deciding on a punishment. Suspension as a punishment should be laid down in an agreement or in the work rules with precise reasons and degrees. Suspension while deciding on a punishment is used, for example, when the employee is being prosecuted for a crime which would justify a serious punishment – such as disciplinary discharge – and the employer waits to hear the decision of the Court. The legal effect of a suspension as a punishment is highly controversial, especially when it is accompanied by a wage decrease or wage cut. The Courts will examine the appropriateness of each suspension, taking into account the seriousness of the reason, the length of the period and also whether or not the wages have been decreased or cut.

Chapter VI. The Termination of the Individual Labour Contract

§1. Job Security in General

138. Article 27, Sect. 1 of the Constitution provides the right to work as a fundamental human right of the Japanese people. This is interpreted as meaning that the Government has a political obligation to try and provide jobs for all those who are willing to work. The obligation to work imposed by the same provision is interpreted as meaning that, with regard to those who are able to work but who do not want to, the Government has no obligation to assure them of the 'wholesome and cultured life' which is guaranteed by Art. 25 of the Constitution. Under Art. 27, the Government should take the necessary measures to guarantee jobs: such as public employment agencies, public works to provide work for the unemployed, a training scheme to improve the workers' chances of getting better jobs and finally an unemployment insurance scheme. All these measures are put into effect by a number of laws – including the Employment Measures Law of 1966, Employment Security Law of 1947, Emergency Unemployment Countermeasures Law of 1949, Occupational Training Law of 1969, Employment Insurance Law of 1974 and other special laws to promote the employment of the old and the handicapped and to give job security to workers in certain industries such as the ports and coal-mining – and by orders of the Labour Ministry to provide re-training benefits for workers who have been dismissed from depressed industries such as textiles, the ports and fishing.

139. Apart from the above-mentioned Governmental obligation, Art. 27 of the Constitution is also interpreted so as to make the promotion of job security a matter of public order. Thus, the decisions of the Courts often proclaim that the employer must respect this public order and not abuse his right of dismissal. Reflecting the extraordinary nature of the dismissal of regular employees under the life-time employment system, the Courts have developed a rather strict attitude towards dismissal, often requiring 'just cause' even for dismissal with notice. Another important characteristic of the law on dismissal in Japan is that the Courts always declare the dismissal null and void and order the continuance of the employment contract whenever they find it to be illegal. The result is that the dismissed employee is always reinstated unless he prefers to claim damages instead. Partly because of the life-time employment system (under which the second job is usually inferior to the first), and partly because of the sentimentality of the employees who neglect their best economic interests in order to save face, in most cases the dismissed employee will seek to go back to his former working place unless the matter has been settled by conciliation. But, quite often, reinstated workers do not remain long in their old jobs because of the damage done to their personal relationships with the management and their former colleagues. So, the wisdom of this legal principle is not completely beyond doubt, especially given the changing labour market situation which means that dismissed workers can in fact find better jobs.

§2. Ending the Contract other than by Dismissal

140. The contract of employment is regarded as a personal contract, and the death of the employee or, in the case of an individual employer, of the employer, brings the contract automatically to an end. In the case of a corporate employer, the death of the representative does not affect the contractual relationship. Only the dissolution of the legal person, that is the company will end the contract. However, a change in the legal form of the corporate employer – from company to partnership or individual owner – does not affect the contract. If there is a merger of companies opinion is divided, but the majority agree that the contract passes to the new company established by the merger or to the company which has taken over. A change of name, form or even ownership of the enterprise done in order to avoid the application of the legal restrictions on dismissal is denied its effect by the Courts as long as they can find an actual successor to the enterprise. In the same way, the dissolution of the legal person as an employer can also be regarded as intentional avoidance of the law, and the Courts will declare the continuance of the contract with the real successor if there is one.

141. The bankruptcy or insolvency of the employer does not automatically terminate the contract. There is still the possibility of the enterprise continuing to exist throughout the liquidation process until the final dissolution or end of the business; and even surviving, with the help of procedures such as the 'concordat judiciaire'. Therefore, the contract can continue to exist until the very end of the business unless the employer dismisses the employees with notice before this time.

142. The contract for a definite period will automatically come to an end when the period is up; but Art. 21 of the Labour Standards Law has amended this civil law principle as we have already explained in Chapter I, §2. II. Thus, in order to terminate the contract for a definite period which has continued for longer than the period prescribed by law for each kind of contract, the employer must give 30 days' notice.

§3. Termination by the Employee or by Agreement

143. Termination of the contract by the employee is regulated by civil law principles only. Thus, he is free to terminate the contract with less than 30 days' notice depending on the type of contract, or without any notice if there is an 'inevitable reason' (see Chapter I, §2. I). A termination to which both parties agree is not a dismissal, and therefore not regulated by the restrictions on dismissal in the Labour Standards Law. However, because of the unequal standing of employer and employee, it is quite possible that an agreement has in fact been forced on the employee by the employer. For this reason the Courts often regard the termination of the contract as a mere formality to avoid the restrictions on dismissal, and apply the rules relating to dismissal regardless.

144. Whether or not an agreement to terminate the contract can be concluded beforehand is a controversial question. For instance, the work rules often stipulate that the contract will automatically end when retirement age is reached. One judgment has laid down that in such a case dismissal or agreement to terminate is not necessary. Since the contract of employment until retirement age is not a contract for a definite period (if it was it would contradict the prohibition on concluding a contract for a definite period of longer than one year), this interpretation is not completely beyond doubt. Of course, as the employee must be well aware of the possibility of being dismissed when he reaches retirement age, it is perhaps reasonable to say that no notice is needed. However, since (in cases other than those involving retirement age) the intention of an advance agreement to terminate the contract is always somewhat dubious, and may possibly be to avoid the legal restrictions on dismissal, it is reasonable to deny the legal effect of such an agreement and to require notice.

§4. Dismissal with Notice

145. No special form of notice is required – it can be given orally or in writing. But because of the lack of a required form the Courts often have a difficult task in ascertaining the date of the notice. In order to avoid trouble, employers are recommended to give notice in writing with the reason for the dismissal. Obscure reasons may also cause trouble if the legal effect of the dismissal is ever challenged (see §6). Although the period of notice can be reduced by paying an equivalent amount of wages, the effect of the shorter notice is controversial. For instance, when an employer dismisses an employee without either giving notice or paying the average wages for 30 days' work, is such a dismissal definitely null and void or is the contract terminated after 30 days and the employee only entitled to claim 30 days' wages? Opinions differ, but the leading theory and the legal precedents seem inclined to give the employee the right to choose; namely, he can either claim 30 days' wages or else argue that the dismissal is without legal effect.

146. The Labour Standards Law does not require any reason to be given for dismissal with 30 days' notice. However, legal precedent has established a rather strict rule concerning the reasons for dismissal, regardless of whether or not notice has been given. This problem will be discussed later, when we consider the reasons for dismissal in general (see §6).

§5. Dismissal without Notice

147. The Labour Standards Law provides that the employer need not give notice when the employee has been personally responsible for bringing about the reason for dismissal, or when the continuance of his enterprise has been made impossible by some natural calamity or other inevitable reason. Here the 'inevitable reason' is interpreted as meaning a reason equivalent to a natural calamity: that is, similar to an act of God. It must be caused by something outside the employer's control which happened so suddenly that he had no chance of avoiding it under normal circumstances and thus had no time to give notice. For instance, a sawmill which has lost its stock of wood in a flood and is unable to get any more wood in the near future is obviously forced to close down either partly or completely. But if the employer cannot get wood because of his own bad management then he must give notice before dismissing his employees. A redundancy caused by a power cut is not regarded as an 'inevitable cause'. The employer must first obtain the approval of the Labour Standards Office. This approval does not necessarily guarantee the legality of the dismissal, but a dismissal without approval is null and void. The legality of a dismissal without notice will be re-evaluated by the Courts in the final analysis if it is ever challenged.

§6. Reasons for Dismissal – 'Just Cause', Abusive Dismissal

148. The civil law requires an 'unavoidable reason' to terminate an employment contract without notice. The Labour Standards Law introduced an even tighter restriction on dismissal by permitting it without notice only when there is an 'inevitable cause'; which as we have already seen is close to an act of God. But so far no written law requires any reason for dismissal with notice. However, legal theory has also established some very strict rules concerning dismissal with notice. The legal reasoning behind these rules should be examined separately for individual dismissal and collective dismissal.

I. Individual Dismissal

149. When the legal effect of an individual is challenged in Court the worker's claim is either that the dismissal infringes his fundamental human rights because it is based on his political or religious thought, creed or activity, union activity, sex, social status or race; or else that the dismissal is an abuse of the employer's right of dismissal. In either case, in order to refute the worker's argument, the employer is forced to submit some reasonable cause for dismissal which will eventually satisfy the Court. Thus, the Court normally seeks to find out whether there is a reasonable cause or 'just cause' as it is often called. The actual legal process operates in such a way that the Court, after hearing both sides' arguments and examining the evidence and any witnesses, can evaluate which is more plausible – the worker's claim of illegal dismissal or the employer's claim of just cause. In the case of abusiveness, the Courts also evaluate the claims made by both sides: just cause raised by the employer on the one hand, and its denial and the seriousness of the effect of the dismisal on the worker's life on the other hand. In both cases, theoretically speaking, the burden of proof is on the worker according to the normal rules of civil law procedure. But, since it is very difficult to prove someone's intentions, the

Courts often switch this burden of proof from the worker to the employer if some circumstantial evidence is submitted. For instance, if the evidence shows that the employer is hostile towards a certain religious creed, the unions or a political party, the Court will decide that the dismissal was for this reason unless the employer can convince it that the dismissal was in fact for a good reason; such as the serious misconduct of the employee or his extraordinarily bad record at work.

150. The Courts have adopted a rather strict attitude towards admitting the existence of a 'just cause'. From the general trend of the legal precedents it would seem that Japanese employers are not allowed to dismiss workers just because of their inefficiency, laziness or any minor misconduct. The following are a few examples of cases in which dismissals – mostly disciplinary ones – have been declared null and void either because of the lack of a 'just cause' or because of abusiveness. (Of course their legality is to be judged according to all the various elements of the particular case and not merely by looking at the reasons given by the employers; so these examples simply serve to suggest the overall trend of the legal decisions and generalisation must be strictly avoided.) The dismissal of an employee for watching a tennis match during working hours and sleeping during the night-shift was declared to be an abusive dismissal. The dismissal of an employee who was given a 6 month suspended sentence for drunken driving was declared null and void. The dismissal of a hospital employee for obscene behaviour towards a nurse while on a company recreation trip was declared to be an abusive dismissal. In a number of cases the dismissals of employees arrested because of activities such as street demonstrations have been declared null and void. The dismissal of a maintenance worker for selling wheels which belonged to the company was also declared to be abusive.

II. Collective Dismissal

151. While there are no special regulations governing collective dismissals as such, the Government has introduced a number of laws and orders to assist those workers made redundant because the industry in which they work is in decline. In fact the Courts have been applying almost the same logic as that which they developed to deal with individual dismissal, although because of the different context the results are somewhat problematical. The Court will again weigh both parties' arguments = the seriousness of the effect of the dismissal on the workers' lives – which is beyond doubt – on the one hand, and on the other necessity of dismissing a certain number of employees because of a decline in business. But the evaluation of business conditions is not an easy task for a court of law; and, furthermore, it is rather absurd for the Court to say that the employer should avoid closing the plant or reducing the scale of business. Thus, in the course of the legal process the Court will have to accept the necessity of a certain number of dismissals and merely scrutinise the appropriateness of the selection of the workers who are to be dismissed. In deciding on this point the Court is faced with two rather contradictory considerations. One reasonable basis for selection might be the employer's interest in dismissing his less efficient employees, while at the same time preferring to dismiss his most expensive employees: in the Japanese context this means older workers with long service who may have large families. Another possible way is to choose those employees on whom the effect of dismissal will not be so serious: namely younger, preferably single, employees who have a better chance of finding a similar job elsewhere. The Courts seem to have been applying these contradictory standards rather at random, using their discretion to judge the various factors involved in each particular case. Perhaps this is one of the fields in which some legislation is now needed.

§7. Redundancy

152. Aside from the regulations on collective dismissals which were developed mainly by the law courts, in the 1970's the Government introduced a number of pieces of legislation to protect workers from redundancy and to promote re-training and re-employment of those hit by the recession which followed the oil crisis. In 1974 the Government replaced the 30 year old Unemployment Insurance System with the Employment Insurance System which introduced the Employment Adjustment Grant Scheme. This Scheme was integrated into the Employment Stabilisation Fund System which was established in 1977 and aims to assist redundant workers by providing grants to employers who introduce various measures to avoid redundancy.

I. Employment Stabilisation Fund System

153. The Employment Stabilisation Fund System consists of the Employment Stabilisation Service and the Employment Stabilisation Fund. The former aims to prevent unemployment and to stabilise employment by subsidising such employment adjustment measures as temporary lay-offs (temporary suspension from work with wages paid), education, training and others, which are often taken by enterprises on behalf of their redundant workers during production adjustment periods resulting from cutbacks in operations due to business fluctuations or changes in the industrial structure. The Employment Stabilisation Fund provides the funds for the effective operation of the above services. Considering that the Employment Stabilisation Service will be greatly affected by business fluctuations, and that large sums will therefore be paid out during recessions while little will be spent during boom times, an Employment Stabilisation Fund was set up in the Labour Insurance Special Account (Employment Accounts). The amount of money needed for the Service is accumulated in this Fund, to be effectively appropriated for the Service when necessary.

154. Available under the Employment Stabilisation Service are the following:

1. Employment Adjustment Services in the Case of Business Fluctuations

If employers in industries designated by the Minister of Labour are compelled to minimise business operations due to business fluctuations or for other economic reasons, but conduct temporary lay-offs (temporary suspension from work with wages paid) and provide education and/or training for their employees, subsidies will be granted as follows:

(1) Employment Adjustment Grant: Employers who have paid a non-duty allowance to their workers who were laid-off temporarily under a labour-management agreement concerning the suspension of business will be granted half of the non-duty allowance ($\frac{2}{3}$ for smaller enterprises) for up to 75 days.

(2) Training Adjustment Grant: Employers who, under a labour-management agreement, have conducted education or training for their employees while paying normal wages during the business adjustment period will be granted half of the normal wages ($\frac{2}{3}$ for smaller enterprises) for up to 75 days.

(3) Subsidy for Training Adjustment Expenses: Employers who have conducted the above-mentioned education or training at their own expense will be provided with a grant of 480 Yen a day (610 Yen for statutory vocational training).

2. Employment Adjustment Services in the Case of Business Conversions

Subsidies will be granted to employers in industries designated by the Minister of Labour who have been compelled to convert their businesses or to minimise business operations due to a change in industrial structure or for other economic reasons and who conduct temporary lay-offs, provide education and/or training and transfer their employees. There are four kinds of subsidies:

(1) Training Grant in the Case of Business Conversion;
(2) Subsidy for Training Expenses in the Case of Business Conversion;
(3) Non-duty Grant in the Case of Business Conversion; and
(4) Transfer Grant in the Case of Business Conversion.

II. Measures for Employment Opportunity Creation

155. Even those measures mentioned above are not sufficient to enable all unemployed workers to find new employment. The following measures to create job opportunities are also available.

1. Employment Creation Grant for Middle-aged and Older Workers

In order to develop employment opportunities for middle-aged and older workers, a grant will be allowed to employers who have employed the said workers for certain periods designated by the Minister of Labour depending on business fluctuations and who have increased the number of these workers in terms of the total number of their employees. Namely, eligible employers will be granted an amount of money equivalent to $\frac{1}{2}$ of normal wages ($\frac{2}{3}$ for medium and small enterprises) for the first 3 months of employment in the case of workers aged 45–55 years and for the first 6 months of employment in the case of those aged 55–65 years.

2. Employment Promotion Subsidy Scheme

To enable workers to find the work most suited to their abilities, and to make effective use of manpower, three kinds of subsidies are made available as follows:

(1) Subsidies based on the Employment Structure Improvement Service under the Employment Insurance System;
(2) Employment Promotion Subsidies based on the Employment Measures Law of 1966; and
(3) Employment Promotion Subsidies based on the Law concerning Temporary Measures for Displaced Coal Miners of 1959, amended in 1977. In addition, there is also the 'Employment Promotion Subsidy for Workers Displaced from Specific Depressed Industries' and the 'Employment Promotion Subsidy for Displaced Workers due to Business Conversion and so forth'. If employers have engaged displaced workers then $\frac{1}{2}$ of normal wages ($\frac{2}{3}$ for middle-sized and small enterprises) will be granted so as to promote the employment of the displaced workers concerned.

III. Specific Employment Measures

156. Measures to promote the employment of specific groups of workers were also introduced during the 1970's.

1. Measures for Middle-aged and Older Workers

In 1976 the Law concerning Special Measures for Employment Promotion for Middle-aged and Older Persons of 1971 was revised, and a new employment quota system for older workers was established to replace the one formerly stipulated. According to the newly established employment quota system, employers are obliged to make efforts to employ a number of such workers (aged 55 and over) more than equivalent to the quota of 6 per cent (enacted from 1 October 1976). To promote the employment of middle-aged and older workers, employers in establishments which employ such workers will be granted various benefits such as:

(1) The Employment Promotion Subsidy for Middle-aged and Older Workers;
(2) In the case of employing these workers during a period of recession, the Employment Creation Grant for Middle-aged and Older Workers; and
(3) In the case of continuing the employment of those who have reached the mandatory retirement age, the Uninterrupted Employment Promotion Subsidy. Further, a low interest loan will be made available for employers who provide workers with the necessary welfare facilities.

2. Measures for Physically Handicapped Persons

Due to the revision of the Physically Handicapped Persons' Employment Promotion Law of 1960 in 1976, the provision concerning employment quotas for such persons – which had called for employers' efforts to achieve quotas –

was revised into an obligatory one, and along with this the Physically Handicapped Persons' Hiring Payment System was newly established (effective from 1 October 1976). Under the Physically Handicapped Persons' Employment Quotas System all employers are obliged to employ a number of such persons more than equivalent to the rate specified by the Ministry of Labour Ordinance (the rate is fixed at 1.5 per cent for private enterprises, 1.8 per cent for special juridical persons, 1.8 per cent for operational government offices and 1.9 per cent for non-operational government offices). The Ministry of Labour is now making every possible effort in its guidance toward achievement of the mandatory employment quotas. In an attempt to promote employment, especially in the private sector and with special juridical persons where the employment record is extremely poor, the Ministry has required them to draw up a 'Programme concerning the Employment of Physically Handicapped Persons'. Along with the above System, the Physically Handicapped Persons' Hiring Payment System has also been established to adjust the imbalanced expenses incurred by employing handicapped workers and to alleviate the financial burdens shouldered by employers by providing the facilities and equipment necessary for such workers. Under this System:

(1) Employers who do not comply with the mandatory quotas will be fined and the amount accumulated in the fund;
(2) The fund will be appropriated for the 'Physically Handicapped Persons' Employment Adjustment Grant' ('Incentive Pay' for medium and small enterprises), which will be provided to employers who have exceeded mandatory quotas; and
(3) Some kinds of subsidies will be granted to employers who provide the new facilities and equipment necessary.

In stepped-up efforts to promote the employment of physically and mentally handicapped persons financial assistance is extended to employers as follows:

(1) Employers who hire such persons will be granted the Employment Promotion Subsidy for Physically Handicapped Persons.
(2) Employers who hire a large number of handicapped workers will be given the funds necessary for the procurement of buildings, machinery and equipment. Many types of loans are also made available.
(3) Furthermore, these employers will be given favourable taxation treatment, such as reductions in corporation and operation taxes.

§8. Disciplinary Discharge

157. Most work rules stipulate various kinds of disciplinary punishment for violations of management rules and orders. These punishments range from a warning, a reprimand or a reduction in wages to suspension, demotion and finally discharge. As for the legal foundation of the employer's power to impose discipline, different explanations have been given. Some theories find it in the employer's power to order and rule his enterprise, or in the intrinsic power of the head of the enterprise as an institution. However, the relationship between the employer and his employees is essentially a contractual one, and the employer as head of the enterprise can only command his right to order on the basis of a contract, so the leading theories deny the intrinsic power of the employer to discipline his employees and tend to find its legal foundation in the contract. Thus, only when punishments are agreed upon either in the work rules or in a collective agreement may the employer use them to punish his employees. Because of the penal nature of disciplinary punishment the reasons for the punishment and the degree of punishment should always be laid down in precise detail.

158. Among the various kinds of disciplinary punishment disciplinary discharge is, needless to say, the most severe. Furthermore, most work rules lay down that the discharge is without notice and without or with reduced retirement allowances. Such a discharge is treated as dismissal without notice and should thus have to meet the requirements of the Labour Standards Law: namely it must have the approval of the Labour Standards Office and it must have been caused by the employee – which means serious misconduct on his part. As for the retirement allowance, it is usually understood that its reduction or forfeiture is a contractual matter and that there is no problem if there is a provision to this effect.

§9. Early Retirement System

159. An early retirement system is sometimes put into effect for special categories of employees; particularly for women. Such a system applied regardless of sex is legal only in so far as it is reasonable to have early retirement because of the nature of the work or the group of employees. This is, however, very exceptional.

160. As for early retirement for women, this, together with retirement on marriage, has been a rather controversial issue in Japan for several years. Until fairly recently most women workers were temporary employees who expected to retire when they got married. Thus, in Japanese enterprises early retirement or retirement on marriage used to be quite common. Sometimes it was explicitly laid down in the work rules, sometimes an agreement was entered into on starting work or sometimes a subtle agreement existed in practice. However, in recent years, partly because of the rise in the status of women and their emancipation from the traditional morals and any old bias – as well as from the burden of household chores with the development of electrical gadgets – and partly because of the increasing demand for higher living standards caused by rapid economic growth, but mostly because of the great demand for female labour caused by the serious labour shortage in the years before the oil crisis; not only the number of women workers, but also the percentage of married women working and their average age and length of service has increased steadily (see Tables XX and XXI).

TABLE XX

Average Age and Length of Service of Female Employees

	1960	1965	1970	1975	1980	1982
Average Age	26.3	28.1	29.8	33.4	34.8	35.0
Average Length of Service (in years)	4.0	3.9	4.5	5.8	6.1	6.3

Source: Labour Ministry, *Basic Statistical Survey of Wage Structure.*

TABLE XXI

Marital Status of Female Employees (%) in non-Agricultural Industries

Years	Total Female Employees	Unmarried	Married	Divorced and Widowed
1962	100.0(802)	55.2	32.7	12.0
1965	100.0(893)	50.3	38.6	11.1
1970	100.0(1,086)	48.3	41.4	10.3
1975	100.0(1,159)	38.0	51.3	10.8
1980	100.0(1,345)	32.5	57.4	10.0
1982	100.0(1,408)	31.5	58.8	9.7

Source: Bureau of Statistics, Prime Minister's Office, *Survey on Labour Force* (Tokyo: 1962–1982).
( ) = real numbers in ten thousands

161. Reflecting this trend, numerous cases regarding the legality of early retirement and retirement on marriage have been brought before the Courts in recent years. In the overwhelming majority of such cases the Courts have declared the unconstitutionality of both, holding that early retirement for women is against the equality of men and women and that retirement at marriage contradicts this and at the same time infringes the freedom of marriage. The Courts have turned down the employers' argument that women are, on average, less efficient and less committed to the job and are an expensive labour force because of all the protection provided for them by labour law. Their reasoning is that efficiency and commitment should be judged individually and that there is no evidence that women in general are an inferior labour force. The Courts also claim that the protection given to women is justified by their special characteristics and that employers may not treat them unequally because of this; otherwise the very purpose of having a law to protect them would be lost.

§10. Termination of Special Kinds of Employment Contracts

162. The termination of a probationary contract is treated as a dismissal, even at the end of the probationary period, if the period has exceeded 14 days (see Chapter I, §2 and §3). As for the reasons for terminating the contract of a probationary worker, the Courts again adopt a rather restrictive attitude, although it is slightly different from that adopted towards the dismissal of a regular employee because of the very nature of the contract of probation. Namely, since the purpose of probation is to evaluate the worker's suitability as a regular employee of that particular enterprise, the employer should have more freedom of discretion.

163. The strict attitude of the Courts can be explained by the somewhat unusual nature of the Japanese method of recruitment. Especially in the case of regular employees, the enterprises go through a long, careful process of selection before making their final choice. Quite often this process starts in the early autumn – or even the early summer, depending on the individual enterprise – and ends in April when the new school-leavers actually start work. During this period the enterprises announce their recruitment plans, accept written applications, hold a series of tests including evaluation by written application form, written examination and interview, and investigate all the personal factors such as family, friends and relationships, often employing private detectives to do so. Finally, the enterprise will inform those who have passed all the tests that they are nominated as candidates for employment from next April. Considering this very careful selection process, the Courts naturally take the view that a probation period starting from April is rather too much, and that it is not fair if the employer still has unlimited freedom to screen once again before deciding who will finally be employed on a regular basis.

164. Another special problem with arises with regard to this screening process is whether the employer can cancel the relationship with a candidate before his employment starts in April. Several years ago, because of the serious labour shortage, enterprises began to start recruiting earlier in order to get the better workers before other firms got them – since then the decision to take candidates has also tended to be made earlier. Thus, without completing the careful process of investigation, the decision is announced to the candidates; only to be revoked later when the enterprise finds something wrong with a particular candidate. Certain legal problems arise: what is the legal nature of the relationship between this candidate and his employer-to-be? Theories and judicial decisions are divided. Some say that the relationship is a contract in advance with the effect of concluding an employment contract later, and so the candidate is only entitled to receive an indemnity if the Court finds that the cancellation was abusive. Others claim that a special kind of employment contract is concluded when the decision is announced to the candidate, and that the termination should be regarded as a dismissal and thus be subject to the rules governing dismissal. According to this latter view, the candidate can claim employee status if the termination is found to be abusive.

§11. Regulations Regarding the End of the Contract

165. At the end of the labour contract the rights and obligations of both parties are terminated – except for those that have already been realised; that is, the worker's right to wages for the work done and to such things as workman's compensation, and his obligation to return any property belonging to the employer which he used in his work, such as tools or a uniform. Workers also have a certain obligation after the contract has ended to observe the secrets of the employer and to avoid competing against him, which will be described in Chapter VII. Also, the Labour Standards Law imposes a certain obligation on the employer after the contract has ended to protect the worker's interests.

166. The employer must provide a certificate giving details of the worker's period of employment, his occupation, his position in the enterprise and his wages upon the request of the worker at the end of the contract. He shall not insert in the certificate anything which the worker does not require. Furthermore, the employer, in conspiracy with a third party, shall not send any communication or put any secret mark on the certificate indicating the nationality, creed, social status or union activities of the worker with the intention of impending his future employment. (Art. 22 of the Labour Standards Law.) This is the prohibition of the black list. However, the employer may provide certain information about former employees if asked to do so by their new or prospective employers.

167. At the end of the contract the employer shall complete the payment of wages and return whatever reserves, bonds, savings or other funds and valuables he has which belong to the worker within 7 days of the claimant asking for them (the claimant may be the bereaved family of a dead worker) (Art. 23 of the Labour Standards Law). Wages are taken to include retirement allowances.

168. The employer must pay the necessary travelling expenses of the worker who returns home within 14 days of the cancellation of the contract if the worker has cancelled it because of the real working conditions were different from those which were specified before the contract was concluded (Art. 15 of the Labour Standards Law). The employer must also pay the necessary fare in the case of minors under 18 years of age or women who wish to return home within 14 days of dismissal; except if they were responsible for their own dismissal and he has obtained authorisation from the Labour Standards Inspection Office to this effect (Art. 68 of the Labour Standards Law).

Chapter VII. Covenants of Non-Competition, Inventions by Employees

§1. Covenants of Non-Competition

169. The work rules of most companies lay down that retired employees should not make known company secrets acquired during their employment. And some of them also provide that retired employees should not work for or engage in business with companies which are in competition with their previous employers.

170. These provisions raise several legal problems. To some extent they restrict the freedom of choice of work open to retired employees. It is inevitable that employees will acquire a certain knowledge and grasp of techniques during their employment. The courts have held that if such knowledge and techniques are of a universal and general nature within the particular trade or industry, and could be acquired by other employers, then employees should not be prevented from exploiting their accumulated knowledge or grasp of techniques after their retirement. In such a case the restriction will be illegal because it curtails the employee's freedom without just cause. But if the knowledge and techniques are peculiar to the company, and are the specific property of the company, they should be protected as business secrets. In this case the restriction of competition will be justified. However, even if this is so, the restriction should not be for too long. In one case the Court upheld a two year restriction as being reasonable. The Courts will also take other factors into consideration, such as the scope of the restriction in terms of its geographical area and the trade or business in which competition is prohibited.

171. In some companies a reduction in the amount of the retirement allowance is prescribed for those who retire in order to work for another company in the same trade. In one case the work rules provided that retirement allowances would be halved if an employee retired in order to work for another company in the same trade. The company had paid the normal retirement allowance to a particular employee, only to find out later that he was working for another company in the same trade. Thus the original company sued him, claiming that half of the money had to be paid back. The Supreme Court upheld the High Court decision, which repealed the District Court decision. The District Court had held that reducing the retirement allowance was illegal since the provision in the work rules contradicted the provision in the contract governing the amount of indemnity to be paid for breach of the employment contract (Art. 16 of the Labour Standards Law). The work rules did not explicitly prohibit competition, but the reduction in the amount of the retirement allowance provided the amount of indemnity for the breach of the obligation of non-competition implicitly implied. The High Court and the Supreme Court both held that the amount of the retirement allowance was a matter to be decided by the company for each category of employee as one of their working conditions. According to the Supreme Court, a restriction on the employment of a retired employee by another company in the same trade is not illegal as an unreasonable restriction on the freedom of work if it is for a reasonable length of time.

§2. Inventions by Employees

172. There are no special regulations concerning inventions by employees, although the work rules of many companies provide for commendations for them. An invention is just one of the reasons for a commendation; others are long service, a special contribution to the company and good conduct. The company gives a testimonial – a small amount of money or a gift, special promotion or extra holidays. The amount of money usually given ranges from 100,000 Yen to 2,000 Yen (nearly $500 to only $10) depending on the reasons for the commendation and the company. Besides commendations, the work rules of some companies cover the rights to inventions. Most of them provide that the company has these legal rights to begin with, or else that the employee must transfer them to the company if he made the invention within the scope of his job in the company. Some work rules even provide that in the case of inventions by employees which are connected with their jobs, although not directly or specifically, the company will get priority in any negotiations if the employee wishes to trade his rights. The company shall apply for the registration of the patent, copyright or other legal rights to the invention and pay compensation to the employee. The amount of compensation provided for in the work rules is usually quite small – ranging from about 2,000 Yen to 200,000 Yen. Sometimes it is stipulated that the company must make some additional payment which depends on the actual utilisation of the invention.

173. Because of the technological development of modern industry, and the growing number and importance of inventions by employees in an age of organised industry, the present lack of protective legislation in respect of an employee's rights to his own inventions is a serious legal problem. But theory and case law in this area are still very underdeveloped. The present trend, both in the work rules and in practice, is based on the consideration that in normal cases inventions come about with the employee using the company's facilities, tools, and materials and having the co-operation of the other employees; all of which happens during working hours for which the company is paying. However, at the same time, the invention might really be a result of the employee's own ability and efforts. Thus, the problem is to balance the weight of the company's contribution against that of the employee's contribution. The provisions in the work rules assume the normal situation – in which the value of the invention is not very great and the company's contribution has been the major factor– but special legilsation is certainly needed to protect the employee in cases where the value of the invention is enormous and the employee's contribution has been a major factor.

Part II. Collective Labour Relations

174. The system of collective labour relations in Japan is shaped by history on the one hand and by the structure of labour law on the other. Historically, the Japanese trade unions of today are products of the post-war period; the pre-war unions having been completely destroyed during the war by the military government. After the second World War unions were organised with the active encouragement of the Occupational Forces. This does not necessarily mean that the unions were organised solely on the initiative of the public authority, but it is undeniable that the unions were organised without any great difficulty and have the weaknesses which are characteristic of organisations born without a struggle. The easy birth gave an air of fragility and easy-goingness to union organisation in Japan which has still not been completely overcome. Legally, the rights to organise, to bargain and to act collectively were provided by the Constitution as fundamental human rights. This constitutional guarantee of workers' rights, including the right to bargain, is almost unknown in other countries. In fact it gave too much protection to the unions, which, together with the rather excessive protection provided for them by labour law, may perhaps have resulted in increasing the fragility of union organisation orginally caused by the historical factors we have already mentioned.

175. Collective labour law in Japan has its foundation in the three fundamental workers' rights. Thus, it is divided into the law regarding trade union organisation, the law of collective bargaining and the law governing action in the course of disputes. the constitutional guarantee of these rights reveals another characteristic of Japanese collective labour law: that is, that almost everything concerning union organisation, bargaining or labour disputes comes under the jurisdiction of the Courts. This poses two obvious problems. First, there is no system of labour courts in Japan and so the ordinary Courts, which are not specialised in labour problems, have to handle collective labour relations – a subject which by its nature is not well suited to the traditional legal approach. Secondly, the fact that there is a Labour Relations Commission system which deals with unfair labour practices and dispute settlement in a semi-judicial way raises difficult problems with regard to the overlapping jurisdictions of the Commissions and the Courts in certain fields.

Chapter I. The Right to Organise

§1. Bona Fide Trade Unions and Qualified Unions

176. The right to organise is guaranteed for all workers. This means that all workers may organise unions according to their own wishes in terms of the type of organisation, organisational principles and policies. These workers' organisations will be recognised as having the right to organise if their purpose is to promote the workers' interests against the employers, and if they are independent of the employers as well as the Government; in other words, in so far as they are *unions*, rather than workers' political parties or workers' co-operative societies, and are not company-dominated or mere Government puppets. Such bona fide trade unions enjoy the three rights guaranteed by the Constitution and are thus legally entitled to organise, bargain and act collectively. Their rights in this respect are safeguarded by the Courts.

177. The Trade Union Law defines 'unions' as follows: trade unions are organisations or federations organised autonomously by the workers for the main purpose of maintaining and improving their economic status and which,

1. do not accept as members persons such as directors of enterprises and employees at supervisory level with responsibility for personnel management or access to confidential information concerning personnel management;
2. do not receive financial support from the employers, with the exception of the wages of union representatives during bargaining or negotiations and the employer's contribution to the union's welfare fund;
3. do not aim solely to provide mutual aid or to do other welfare work;
4. do not aim principally to carry on a political or a social movement.

178. Unions which qualify under the Trade Union Law must include the following provisions in their constitutions in order to be entitled to participate in the formal procedures provided by the law and to avail themselves of the remedies given by it,

1. members of the union, unless it is a federated one, shall have the right to participate in all union affairs and the right to equal treatment;
2. nobody shall be refused membership of the union because of his race, religion, sex, social status or family origin;
3. The officers of the union, unless it is a federated one, shall be elected by direct secret ballot of the members, and the officers of federations or national unions shall be elected by direct secret ballot of the delegates elected by direct secret ballot of the members;
4. a general meeting shall be held at least once a year;
5. the financial report shall be made public to the members at least once a year, together with a certification of accuracy from a professional competent auditor appointed by the members;
6. no strike action shall be started without the agreement of a majority of the members in a direct secret ballot or, in the case of a federation or national

union, of the delegates elected by a direct secret ballot of all the members;
7. no constitution shall be revised without the agreement of a majority of the members in a direct secret ballot or, in the case of a federation or national union, of the delegates elected by a direct secret ballot of all the members.

'Qualified' unions are entitled to participate in the procedures and avail themselves of the remedies provided by the Trade Union Law:

1. they are qualified to be registered and to acquire a legal personality,
2. registered unions are granted exemption from tax,
3. they are entitled to recommend labour members for the Labour Relations Commissions,
4. they are entitled to file complaints of unfair labour practice against employers,
5. they are entitled to request the extension of the effect of collective agreements.

179. Although they do not have access to these procedures and remedies, all bona fide unions enjoy other privileges such as exemption from civil and criminal liability with regard to their legal activities (including strike action), the ability to conclude collective agreements with full legal effect and so on.

§2. Freedom of Association and the Right to Organise

180. Freedom of association is guaranteed to all Japanese people, while the right to organise is guaranteed to workers in addition to the general guarantee of freedom of association. The right to organise is interpreted as guaranteeing something more than the simple freedom to organise a union, since it is distinguished from simple freedom from state power as one of the fundamental human rights peculiar to the new type of constitutions which came into being after the Second World War and which were modelled on the 1918 Weimar Constitution in Germany – the so-called constitutions of the 'social welfare state'. Firstly, while freedom of association can be restricted or abandoned by agreement between private persons, the right to organise is not to be restricted by such an agreement. Thus, all agreements to restrict the right to organise, for example yellow-dog contracts, are null and void as a violation of the right to organise even if the worker had agreed to them. Secondly, while Government interference with personal freedom is unconstitutional, and all legislative and administrative steps in this direction are deemed to be illegal, so also is Government interference with union freedom regarded as being illegal and thus null and void. Furthermore, intervention by private persons in the unions' right to organise is also regarded as being illegal, and as a tort gives rise to a right to indemnity. In this sense the right to organise is almost fully recognised as a civil law right in Japanese legal theory. Thirdly, the Government not only has to abstain from violating the unions' freedom but has also, more positively, to take the steps necessary to promote union organisation. For instance, the unfair labour practice system (see Chapter VI) is seen as one of the necessary steps required by the constitutional guarantee of the right to organise. Finally, while freedom of association should include the freedom *not* to join an association, the right to organise is interpreted as making union security arrangements legal. The legal effect of union security raises some rather complicated problems and needs detailed examination – which it will receive in the next section.

§3. The Right to Organise and Union Security

181. Union security arrangements – which most frequently take the form of union shop clauses in Japan since others such as the closed shop, the agency shop and the maintenance of membership are very rare or almost unknown – are regarded as part of the right to organise and are quite legal. However, in practice many complicated legal problems arise regarding their use. The most commonly held view is that the right to organise means only a positive right to organise and the negative right, that is, the freedom to refrain from joining a union, is not guaranteed. On the other hand, since the right to organise is guaranteed to all workers and thus to any bona fide union, if workers who have been expelled or who have seceded from a union with union security organise their own union or join another union their dismissals in implementation of the union security arrangement will be regarded as illegal for violating the right to organise. Thus, quite often union security does not work effectively in the most crucial cases – such as when there is a split in the union organisation.

182. Current legal theory tends to deny the negative right to organise, and so union security is recognised as having full effect with regard to the unorganised. Of course this will mean a conflict between the right of the union to organise and the freedom of individuals who hold strong political or religious beliefs. Union security also causes problems if the union denies equal treatment to all members or the equal right to join regardless of the individual's creed, race, nationality, sex or social status. The dominant legal theory and legal precedent both regard the expulsion of members, or the refusal to admit them, as violating their fundamental human rights and so as being illegal and null and void; and if the expulsion or refusal of membership is null and void the dismissal effected under a union security arrangements is also null and void.

§4. The Right to Organise and Individual Workers

183. Even forgetting the existence of union security arrangements, the rights of individual workers and the union's right to organise could contradict each other if the union has a certain inclination in the political or religious field and forces its members to follow it; or if it treats its members unequally because of differences in creed, race, nationality, sex or social status. Opinion is divided as to whether the rights of the union or of the individual should be better protected. If the union has a union security arrangement and actually dominates or controls job opportunities in a certain field, it will be regarded not as a purely private association but as a semi-public one. Such unions should be required to respect the fundamental human rights of individuals since they enjoy a strong and influential position. However, unions without union security could also be powerful enough to influence the fate of workers. Unions, especially the 'qualified' ones, send delegates to various committees and commissions, including the Labour Relations Commission. Thus, most unions are regarded as semi-public institutions and are required to respect individual rights and equality.

184. The most frequent example of a conflict between the union's right to organise and the individuals' rights is in the case of union support for a particular political party or a certain candidate in a general or local election, when some of the union members do not agree with the union's policy and do not observe the union's orders in this connection. The union then expels or otherwise penalises these members. The Supreme Court has laid down that although unions are free to take a certain political stand, they may not force their views on their members beyond the limits of peaceful persuasion. This means that any disciplinary penalty imposed by the union, including expulsion, is regarded as unconstitutional and null and void.

§5. The Right to Organise and Relations with the Unions

185. As we mentioned above, every union has the right to organise and to bargain collectively, and as a result of this the employer must bargain with every union which demands to bargain with him. Thus, in Japan, a system of exclusive bargaining is taken as violating the union's right to organise and to bargain. However, since every union has legal status, Japanese employers face a very difficult problem: they must bargain faithfully with all the unions and treat them all equally. If the employer bargains with each union in good faith each bargaining session will have different results for the different unions, and this will go against the principle which prohibits discrimination between workers because of their union affiliation.

186. The orders of the Labour Relations Commissions and the decisions of the Courts are very confused. Some say that the employer infringes the right of the minority union to bargain if he insists that it must accept the results of his bargaining with the majority union; while on the contrary some lay down that members of the minority union should be guaranteed the same working conditions as members of the majority union since otherwise the employer is discriminating against them.

§6. Trade Union Property

187. The registered unions have a legal personality and they undoubtedly enjoy the full legal capacity to hold property in their own names. At the same time, they are liable for all the obligations made in the name of the union and for any torts committed by the union or by the leaders of the union as its legal representatives. In other words, the registered unions are treated as legal persons in exactly the same way as companies or any other legal persons. Unions which are not qualified are regarded as 'voluntary associations without legal personality'. However, a theory has been developed which grants almost the same legal status to such associations as to legal persons; except for the registration of their real estate, cars and so on. The result is that unqualified unions enjoy the almost complete capacity to hold property independently of their members, and their liability does not reach individual members beyond their contributions to the unions.

188. So, regardless of their legal personality, all unions in Japan are recognised as owning their own property independently of their members. Therefore, the members have no share in the union's property and members who have seceded or who have been expelled have no claims over this property. Of course it is obvious that difficult legal problems may be brought into being by a split in the union organisation. Theoretically speaking, judging from the description given above of the legal character of the union's property, we can say that the legitimate successor to the former union has full rights to all of the property. However, in practice, two problems arise. Firstly, it is not always easy to decide which is the legitimate successor. Secondly, is it fair to permit a minority union to succeed just because it is found to be legitimate, while in fact a break-away union organises the overwhelming majority of the former union's members? In answer to this the Courts have sometimes laid down that the property should be divided in accordance with the number of members in both unions. This solution might sound quite reasonable, but there is still a problem: when should the numbers be calculated, on the day of the split or on the last day of the hearing? Often, in the first stages of the split, only a small number of members secede and organise another union; but after this the numbers will gradually grow. Most Courts now calculate the numbers on the date on which the hearing closes. The Supreme Court held in one case that members who had seceded had no right to the union's property whether they had organised another union or not.

§7. Internal Union Affairs and Members' Rights

189. The constitution and the rules of the union establish rights and obligations between the union and its members, and between the members themselves. Japanese courts have not hesitated to interfere in the internal affairs of unions in the interests of public order. This means that if there has been any breach of the constitution or of the rules they will declare the action to be illegal and null and void. Thus, the unions' constitutions and rules are treated as legal norms as long as they do not contradict public order. Public order means the rule of democracy and equality, and so any rules and constitutions which do not give equal rights to participate in union activities and an equal vote to all members are deemed to be null and void. Furthermore, all action, including decisions (for instance, the disciplinary punishment of members), taken without fulfilling democratic principles (for instance, taken without giving the member who is being disciplined any chance to defend himself), are null and void.

§8. Trade Union Freedom in Japan and the ILO Conventions

190. Japan has ratified both Convention 87 (1948) and Convention 98 (1949). The problems which the Government experienced during the process of ratification of Convention 87 in 1966 stemmed from provisions in the Public Corporations and National Labour Relations Law and the Local Public Enterprise Labour Relations Law which disqualified those unions which accepted as members, or elected as leaders, workers who were not employed by one of the public corporations or public enterprises. The unions in the public sector suffered from the Government policy of refusing to bargain with unions whose leaders had been dismissed because of prohibited strike action, which was based on these provisions. The unions appealed to various ILO agencies, including the Committee on Freedom of Association and the Committee on the Application of Conventions and Recommendations. Finally, the Japanese Government abolished the provisions which contradicted Convention 87 and ratified it after the Committee on Freedom of Association visited Japan to investigate and conciliate the case in 1965.[1]

1. ILO, 'Report of the Fact-Finding and Conciliation Commission on Freedom of Association Concerning Persons Employed in the Public Sector in Japan', (Dreyer Report), ILO Official Bulletin, Vol. 49, No. 1, Jan. 1966, Special Supplement.

Chapter II. The Trade Unions and Employers' Associations

§1. The Trade Unions

191. Today nearly 34 per cent of all employed persons in Japan are organised. However, the organisation rate is uneven in different industries and sizes of enterprise (see Table XXII). Among the different industries the organisation rate is lowest in the wholesale and retail trades where small stores predominate and highest in the Government service, which is very characteristic of Japanese industrial relations. The unions in the public sector used to be very politically motivated and worked for radical campaigns such as the campaign against the US 'imperialist' foreign policy. Including the public sector, most of the industries with a high percentage rate of organisation, such as finance, insurance, transportation, communications and electricity and gas supply, are dominated by larger enterprises whose employees are predominantly white-collar. Table XXIII shows that the majority of organised labour works in enterprises with 1,000 or more employees, while those working in smaller enterprises with less than 100 employees make up a definite minority. Table XXIV shows that the organisation rate in larger enterprises with more than 500 employees is more than 60 per cent, while in enterprises with less than 30 employees it is only 3.1 per cent.

Table XXII

Union Membership by Industry 1983

Industry	Number of Trade Union Members (1,000 persons)	Estimated Organisation Rate (%)
All Industries	12,520	29.7
Agriculture, Forestry, Fisheries & Marine Products	82	16.4
Mining	46	41.7
Construction	780	18.6
Manufacturing	4,132	35.8
Wholesaling & Retailing	851	9.7
Finance, Insurance & Real Estate	1,020	49.5
Transportation & Communication	1,983	59.6
Electricity, Gas, Water, & Heat Supply	237	64.0
Service	1,688	18.8
Governmental Service	1,499	73.8
Other Industries	201	–

Source: Ministry of Labour Basic Survey of Trade Unions, 1984.

TABLE XXIII

Number of Trade Unions and Membership by Size of Firm

Number Employees	Number of Unions 1981	Number of Unions 1982	Number of Union Members (1,000 persons) 1981	Number of Union Members (1,000 persons) 1982	Percentage Composition (%) in 1982
Total	54,701	55,124	8,740	8,840	100.0
1,000 or more	15,223	15,156	4,730	4,983	56.4
300–999	7,524	7,639	1,398	1,417	16.0
100–299	10,570	10,757	1,027	1,043	11.8
30–99	12,604	12,597	466	463	5.2
29 or less	5,799	5,775	67	69	0.8
Others	2,981	3,000	853	865	9.8

Note: Others includes unions organised by employees or more than 2 firms including one-man enterprises) and unions in enterprises of unknown sizes.
Source: Ministry of Labour Basic Survey of Trade Unions, 1982.

TABLE XXIV

Estimated rate of organisation by size of enterprise in the private sector (1963–80)

Size of Enterprise	1963	1966	1972	1980	
Total	26.7	28.3	28.0	24.7	(%)
500 or more employees	61.3	63.0	63.6	62.0	
100–499	37.6	33.5	31.5	28.8	
30–99	10.4	9.8	9.0	8.1	
29 or less	3.1	4.9	3.4	3.1	

Source: Japan Productivity Centre, Practical Labour Statistics, (Tokyo, 1981).

192. Most trade unions, except the federations, are organised on an enterprise basis. Table XXV shows that the craft and industrial unions are minority unions, both in terms of numbers of unions and in terms of members. However, as we saw in the Introduction, enterprise unions in certain industries organise a number of industrial federations, and these federations and the larger unions – especially those in public enterprises – affiliate directly with one of the national centres. As Table XXVI shows, among the 20 largest unions in Japan (ranking 1, 2, 7, 11, 13 and 19 in the table), 5 are unions organising employees in public corporations or Government enterprise or government employees – in effect they are the enterprise unions of the public sector. These unions are more influential both in numbers of members and financially than some of the industrial federations. As we have already mentioned, there are four national centres of which two, the Sōhyō and the Dōmei, are the most significant in terms of numbers of members (see Table XIV in the Introduction).

TABLE XXV

Number of unions, excluding federations, and their membership by different organisational patterns (1975)

	Number of unions	Number of members
Total	69,333	12,472,000
Enterprise Unions	65,337	11,361,000
Craft Unions	720	169,000
Industrial Unions	1,775	682,000
Others	1,501	259,000

Source: Ministry of Labour Basic Survey of Trade Unions, 1975 (Tokyo: 1976).

193. Within the hierarchy of union organisations the role and functions of the enterprise unions are the most important since most of the bargaining is done at enterprise level. Industrial federations and national centres play an important role in wage determination through the spring offensives, but their control over wage levels in individual enterprises is indirect and incomplete because the spring offensive negotiations only decide the amount or percentage of the wage increase for that year: the basic wage from which the increase is calculated or onto which the increase is added has already been decided by enterprise bargaining. Furthermore, most of the working conditions except wages are decided exclusively by bargaining within each enterprise. While the enterprise unions tend to have more say in deciding on working conditions than do the organisations further up the hierarchy, the industrial federations tend to perform a loose co-ordinating function for their affiliates enabling the exchange of opinions and information. The control of the national centres over their affiliates is much weaker than that of the industrial

TABLE XXVI

The Twenty Largest Trade Unions

Rank	Trade Union (Affiliation)	Occupation or Industry	Membership in 1983 (in thousands)	Rank in 1975	Membership in 1975 (in thousands)
1	Jichiro (Sōhyō)	Local government employees	1,275	1	1,185
2	Nikkyōso (Sōhyō)	Teachers	677	2	634
3	Jidoshasōren (Ind.)	Automobile workers	662	4	524
4	Denkirōren (Chūritsurōren)	Electrical machinery workers	586	3	545
5	Zensen (Dōmei)	Textile workers	479	5	503
6	Seihōrōren (Chūritsurōren)	Life insurance workers	357	8	309
7	Dentsukyōto (Sōhyō)	Tele-communications workers	328	6	325
8	Zenkensōren (Chūritsurōren)	Construction workers	328	11	239
9	Zenkindōmei (Dōmei)	Metal workers	290	7	315
10	Jidosharōren (Dōmei)	Automobile workers	223	16	189
11	Kōkuro (Sōhyō)	National railway workers	224	10	241
12	Tekkōrōren (Sōhyō)	Iron and steel workers	222	9	249
13	Shitetsurōren (Sōhyō)	Private railway workers	201	14	211
14	Zentei (Sōhyō)	Postal workers	182	15	203
15	Zosenjukurōren (Dōmei)	Shipbuilding and heavy machinery workers	177	12	233
16	Shiginren (Ind.)	City bank employees	164	17	182
17	Zenkokukinzoku (Sōhyō)	Metal workers	161	13	214
18	Nihonirokyo (Sōhyō)	Medical workers	142	26	97
19	Kokkororen (Sōhyō)	National government employees	137	–	–
20	Denroyokuroren (Dōmei)	Electric power workers	137	21	133

Source: Japan Productivity Centre, *Practical labour Statistics* (Tokyo, 1984), Ministry of Labour Basic Survey of Trade Unions, 1975, (Tokyo: 1976).

federations, except in the field of ideological, and especially political, activities.

194. As well as defending and promoting their members' economic interests through enterprise bargaining and the spring offensive, the Japanese unions also carry out important social and political functions; including sending delegates to more than 100 Government committees of various kinds – such as the Labour Relations Commissions, the policy making commissions on labour legislation, social insurance, social security and other important public welfare services, price control and so on. Pressure groups are not very strong in Japanese society, with the exception perhaps of the doctors' and farmers' associations, and some recently formed citizens' organisations (for example, anti-pollution groups), and so the trade union influence in politics and society is very significant. So far, however, the unions have not been able to mobilise their influence very effectively because they have been closely committed either to the Socialists or to the Democratic Socialists, both of whom have almost always been minority parties and have never had the chance of implementing their own policies. If the decline of the Liberal Democratic Party continues the influence of the unions in the political field might grow, provided both they and the parties connected with them adopt a more practical and realistic approach and establish and implement some concrete policies in the future.

§2. The Employers' Associations

195. Since bargaining is mostly done at enterprise level, the role, played by the employers' associations in industrial relations is usually restricted to the exchange of information, consultation, the provision of advice and so on. With regard to collective bargaining, they sometimes establish a general policy – especially on wage issues in an attempt to cope with the spring offensive – but such a policy only serves as a guideline and is not binding on the affiliates. At national level, the *Nikkeiren* (Japanese Employers' Association) is the national centre for employers which deals with industrial relations. It is a federation of 47 local associations and 52 industrial associations of employers and has nearly 30,000 employers under its coverage. The main function of these associations is to exchange information and provide advice, but the *Nikkeiren* itself also plays an important role in leading public opinion against the trade unions' national centres in the field of wages, prices and other policies connected with industrial relations. While the *Nikkeiren* mainly organises the rather larger enterprises, the *Shōkōkaigisho* (Chamber of Commerce) and its local branches provide an information and advisory service for smaller enterprises which covers all kinds of business problems and includes industrial relations.

196. The comparative insignificance of the employers' associations in Japan is a direct result of the importance of enterprise bargaining. In addition to this, employers' associations are in a secondary position with regard to the law: for while the right of workers to organise is guaranteed, employers enjoy only the freedom of association. This unequal legal position is indicative of the nature of Japanese labour law, which tends to give rather extensive protection to labour. However, the *Nikkeiren*'s minor role in comparison with the *Keidanren* (Japanese Industrialists' Association) – the role of which is to function as a pressure group representing the interests of business in general – can also be explained by the lack of importance attached to industrial relations by Japanese management in the face of all the other problems they have to cope with.

Chapter III. Institutionalised Relations between Employers and Trade Unions

197. As we have often mentioned, collective bargaining mostly takes place at enterprise level; industrial relations within an enterprise being the most important part of the Japanese industrial relations system. In larger enterprises with more than one plant or work place there are independent unions or branches of the enterprise unions in each of the several work places, and negotiations take place in each of them also. The allocation of bargaining issues and power between the entire enterprise and the individual plants differs according to the history and structure of industrial relations in each enterprise. The degree and type of worker participation in enterprise decision-making also differs from enterprise to enterprise, as do the privileges and benefits which the unions receive from the management. It is only possible here to provide a general perspective on the many diverse industrial relations situations in Japanese enterprises.

§1. The Enterprise Level

198. The 'enterprise union' is a union organised exclusively by the employees in a particular enterprise. Employees who have been dismissed or who have retired will normally lose their membership unless the union is challenging the effectiveness of the dismissal. Temporary employees are not usually admitted to the union. Since all the employees in an enterprise – except temporary employees and supervisory personnel – are entitled to join a union, the enterprise unions in the larger enterprises often organise almost all the eligible employees in the enterprise; and quite often the majority of the employees. In enterprises with more than one plant the enterprise unions will have a 'local' branch in each plant, or sometimes independent plant unions are established in each plant which then organise a federation of plant unions in the enterprise (enterprise federations). However, in practice it is not always very clear whether the plant unions are independent unions or merely branches of the enterprise union. Even when the enterprise union is not a federation, and its members are individuals, the branches in each plant can be independent unions in the sense that they have their own constitutions and rules, their own finance and the authority to make decisions and take action independently of the parent enterprise union. Within a plant, depending on its size, some subdivision of union organisation is often found; generally between the various working divisions such as maintenance, inspection and production. Of course legal problems arise regarding the capacity of 'branches' and 'divisions' of unions to be bargaining parties or to organise acts of dispute including strikes. Since there is no general rule, the Courts decide on capacity according to whether the particular union organisation has independence in the above-mentioned sense.

199. The union will employ a few full-time officers only when it is big enough to be able to afford them. Otherwise part-time officers do the job outside working hours or else the enterprise permits a certain number of union officers to have a certain amount of unpaid leave of absence for union activities. As we have already mentioned, leave of absence with pay is permitted only for the purposes of bargaining and negotiating. Generally speaking, the Japanese unions, being enterprise unions, are in close contact with the rank-and-file on the shop floor and are fairly capable of settling problems on behalf of their members.

200. The union organisations at plant level, if they are majority unions, are responsible for accepting overtime agreements, voicing the employees' opinion of any proposed new work rules and representing the employees on several committees, including those on safety and hygiene in the plant. All these tasks are imposed by various labour laws. And even if they are not majority unions, the employers still have to listen to them if they want to avoid conflict.

201. Of all the organs of decision-making and leadership of the unions, the general meeting of members has the highest authority: it can draft and amend the constitution and rules, decide on the rights and obligations of members and authorise lower organs – including the executive committees and numerous commissions at different levels of union organisation – to carry out special functions. Executive committees, or central committees as they are often called, take care of day to day matters and lead the union between general meetings. Central committees are usually larger than executive committees, are composed of members representing the rank-and-file on a broader basis and are more inclined to co-ordinate the different interests and opinions within the membership than to perform decision-making and leadership functions. Also, when the union organises a strike or some other action, they may establish special committees, often called 'expanded' or 'struggle' committees, to mobilise the rank-and-file and to control them for the leadership.

202. The general pattern of bargaining within the enterprise is as follows:

1. The enterprise union bargains about general working conditions and other issues applicable to all the plants and work places in the enterprise, and concludes agreements for the whole enterprise;
2. the plant branches of the union bargain with the plant managers about issues peculiar to the plant, conclude agreements within the framework of the general agreement and negotiate over matters arising out of the application of the general agreement to the particular situation in the plant; and
3. the divisional branches within the plant have almost the same scope within their own range, except that on this level formal agreements are not generally concluded and informal understandings between the union representatives and the shop-floor supervisors are observed instead – as long as they do not contradict the principles established by the upper levels of institutionalised industrial relations in the enterprise.

203. Strike action or other action is usually decided on by vote at the general meeting and led by the executive committee of the enterprise union. But sometimes the general meeting invests the lower echelons with full power to take action and conclude agreements. Lacking such a decision by the general meeting, the lower echelons are not entitled to do either of these things; unless they are independent in the above-mentioned sense (see para. 198). With regard to concluding collective agreements, most theories tend to accept that the general meeting has the final power to ratify them and give them legal effect – except if decided otherwise by the general meeting.

§2. The Local Level

204. There are several union organisations at regional, prefectural and district level. But most of these bodies serve only to improve communications and the exchange of information between the various unions in a particular area. Their main tasks are educational, political and cultural, and they do not play an important part in bargaining although they do have a role in connection with the spring offensives – that of mobilising and encouraging the unions in the general cause of the struggle. Quite often these organisations are kept merely for the purpose of running political campaigns; for example, to get votes in the local or national elections for the parties and candidates supported by the unions. However, in some areas they have been playing an increasingly important role in local politics, co-operating with other organisations such as citizens' or housewives' organisations in order to protect and promote the interests of the local residents and showing a special interest in problems such as pollution and noise.

§3. The Industrial Level

205. As we mentioned earlier (see §1), the industrial organisations are usually federations of enterprise unions within the different industries. One important exception to this is the Kaiin (All Japan Seamen's Union) which organises over 150 thousand seamen regardless of where they are employed. The bargaining activities of this union are virtually the only example of genuine industrial bargaining. Other exceptions are some general unions which organise workers in small enterprises in certain industries – such as the metal industry – and in small stores of various kinds. On the whole, these unions have not been very successful in bargaining and concluding agreements at the industrial level; except for some success over small areas, they usually just bargain and conclude agreements with each of the enterprises within their jurisdiction. However, they have been successful in getting certain agreements with the same substance covering the majority of workers in a certain district extended to cover all of the employers and their employees.

206. Besides the exceptions mentioned above the industrial federations organise enterprise unions in a number of industries. Some of the most important, in terms of numbers of members, are electrical machinery, automobiles, textiles, insurance, metal, iron and steel, construction, shipbuilding, private railways, banking and transport. However, even these larger federations often come up against enterprise unions which are as strong or even stronger in terms of membership. And, furthermore, the federations' main functions are co-ordinating policy and facilitating the exchange of information: they have no power to control their affiliates. The weakness of the industrial federations is a direct result of the strength of enterprise unionism and the economic background of industrial relations, that is, the life-time employment system and the labour market conditions connected with it. And the dominant position of a few giant enterprise unions over many small enterprise unions in a particular industry is a fairly common situation in the industrial federations. These giant unions tend, quite naturally, to control the federations' policies and activities simply because their larger memberships mean that they can send more delegates to the general meetings and contribute more to the budgets of the federations. The federations have a certain role to play in co-ordinating the targets and strategies – including the steps to be taken and the timing of negotiations and strikes – to be adopted in the case of the spring offensive; but even in this situation their influence in promoting a certain common standard applicable to all the enterprises in the particular industry is far from real. In most cases, because of the significant difference in working conditions between the larger enterprises and the smaller ones, the targets – for example, the amount or rate of the wage increase – are decided differently for two or three groups of differently sized enterprises within the industry.

207. The industrial federations are also involved in the field of politics, supporting certain parties and candidates in the local and national elections by voting and by contributing to their election funds. This practice has, however, caused conflict between factions supporting different parties and has sometimes resulted in unions leaving the federation. Many union leaders are now very keen to change this practice and to introduce the principle of neutrality with regard to party politics; thus gradually uniting the now-divided union fronts into one organisation at national level. Some of the federations have set up industrial commissions under agreements concluded with management industrial associations, and some also send delegates to the commissions on industrial policy established by the Government. The role of the commissions has so far been mainly consultative, but they are likely to become more and more important in the future.

§4. The National Level

208. Of the four national centres, the Sōhyō and the Dōmei have the closest connections with political parties, as we have already mentioned in para. 60. The third most important national centre, the Churitsurōren (Federation of Independent Unions), organises only 10 unions but they are very important ones – such as the Denkirōren (All Japan Federation of Electric Machine Workers' Unions) with over 586 thousand members. Altogether it has 1.4 million workers, slightly less than one-third of the membership of the Sōhyō and 65 per cent of the Dōmei. This centre was originally organised in a rather passive sense to establish contacts between unions not affiliated either to the Sōhyō or to the Dōmei. But today some of the affiliates of the Chūritsurōren and the IMF-JC (Japan Council of Metal Workers' Unions, which organises a number of unions regardless of their affiliation to the national centres), together covering nearly 3 million workers, are trying to establish a united front of unions at national level by denying the commitment of the unions to particular political parties. The Zenminrōkyō, a result of this effort, now organises 4.8 million workers (see para. 62). As well as their political functions, the national centres have, for the last 25 years, played an important part in wage determination through the spring offensive. In the early days of the spring offensive the Sōhyō was the main body organising it, but today most of the unions join the fight and all the national centres participate to some extent in this national event. Since the target of the spring offensive is to increase wages, differences in political ideology are not very significant except in relation to the degree of militancy and aggressiveness displayed. The efforts towards a united front have also, in recent years, relied on the increasingly bread and butter orientation of the trade union movement. However, the economic recession after the oil crisis has had some negative effects on this trend, and it remains to be seen what changes the future will bring.

209. The exact role of the national centres in the spring offensive is not easy to define. The Sōhyō takes the initiative of setting up a committee, called the 'Joint Committee of the Spring Offensive', made up of delegates representing the more important unions participating in the offensive. Through this committee, or in various other more informal ways, the leaders of the national centres and industrial federations reach general agreement about the targets, strategies, schedules for negotiations and strike action and so on. They usually choose one or two industries as pattern setters, taking into account not only their business conditions but also the unions' organisational situation in each of them. In order to arouse public opinion public utilities such as public transport or the postal service are chosen, together with important private industries such as steel or machinery. The conciliation and arbitration procedures of the Central Labour Relations Commission and the Public Corporation and National Enterprise Labour Relations Commission are often utilised to get a favourable settlement. After the wage increases have been decided by groups of major enterprises in the various industries, the unions in smaller enterprises will follow the pattern established by the larger ones – although with some modifications.

Chapter IV. Collective Bargaining

§1. The Significance of Collective Bargaining

210. Since the right to bargain is guaranteed by the Constitution the principle of the superiority of collective bargaining under the autonomy of the parties in industrial relations is firmly established. In 1982 some 9 million employees, which is nearly 90 per cent of the organised labour force, except government employees who are not eligible to bargain collectively, were covered by collective agreements. Besides these formal agreements, there are many written and unwritten agreements at shop floor level which may be more important as regards actual working conditions. As collective agreements have legal binding effect, the law requires a certain formality to attend their conclusion; but at the same time they are agreements between private parties and as such do not require any formal conclusion. The double character of the collective agreement is one of the peculiarities of the Japanese law of collective bargaining. Another peculiarity stems from the fact that while the right to bargain is recognised as a legal right which can be enforced in the Courts, at the same time it is protected by the semi-judicial administrative procedure of the Labour Relations Commission. In describing the law of collective bargaining in Japan it is always a source of some confusion that we can be talking about the same subject but often in the different contexts of these two dimensions. In this chapter we will discuss the general principles which are commonly applicable both to procedures in the Courts and in the Labour Relations Commissions; the problems peculiar to procedure in the Labour Relations Commissions will be discussed in Chapters VI and VII.

§2. The Parties to Collective Bargaining

211. In order to be a party to collective bargaining, and as a result to any collective agreement, the only qualification is to be a bona fide union on the labour side and an employer or employers' organisation on the employers' side. As we have repeatedly pointed out, all bona fide unions have the right to bargain. The employer cannot refuse to bargain with a minority union just because it is a minority union. Theoretically, even a union with only two members is entitled to bargain. If there are a number of unions in a plant the employer has to bargain with them all. However, problems arise concerning the hierarchical order of the union organisation. The union branches or divisions in a plant can be bargaining parties in so far as they are recognised as independent unions in the sense described above (see para. 198). In such cases, in abstract theory the employer has to bargain with all the different levels of the union organisation hierarchy. Of course the unions cannot demand to bargain about exactly the same issue repeatedly or overlappingly at different levels. Without there being any specific arrangement, in principle issues which concern the whole enterprise should be discussed by the enterprise union and the central management, while issues relating to a specific plant or division should be discussed by the appropriate union organisation in that plant or division and the relevant local management or supervisory staff. If, however, the higher echelons of the union have invested the lower levels with the power to bargain, the employer should bargain with the latter; although he may ask the union to regulate the channels or routes of bargaining, keeping them under the control of the central executive in order to avoid confusion and any possible abuse of the right to bargain by the union. So, the employer is entitled to avoid embarrassing situations such as the union demanding to re-open bargaining about the same issue but on a different level when a settlement has already been agreed to on another level.

§3. Bargaining Sessions

212. Various aspects of the bargaining sessions, such as the number of participants, their qualifications and the time, duration and location of the meetings can sometimes cause serious conflict between union and management. Also, the employer can refuse to bargain at all; claiming, for example, that the union delegates have behaved impolitely or violently or have used intimidating language. In fact the employers often try to impose rules on the bargaining sessions, restricting the number of participants from the union and limiting the duration of each session to a few hours. Japanese unions sometimes seem to regard bargaining sessions merely as one of the stages in their confrontation with management, and as occasions for displaying or demonstrating their power by mobilising their members to mass action. They do not distinguish very clearly between bargaining and strike action, seeing both as ways of demonstrating their will to fight (see Chapter V). The question of how far the employer can insist on making rules about such matters, and refuse to bargain until rules are established, is a matter of bargaining in good faith. If the employer is found to be genuinely objecting to the confusion which, judging from the past attitudes of the union, will be caused and not just to be using it as an excuse to avoid bargaining, his refusal is justified.

213. Thus, the Courts and the Labour Relations Commissions may have to decide whether a refusal to bargain because of a lack of rules governing bargaining sessions or because of the union's unreasonable attitude is justifiable; or whether it is a violation of the right to bargain and an unfair labour practice. However, leaving aside these legal questions, it is recommended in practice that the parties to the bargaining process conclude an agreement covering the practical details of their bargaining sessions: the number of participants on both sides, whether not only union leaders but also other persons who are trusted by the union may represent it, whether or not sessions will be held during working hours using the company's facilities, how long the sessions should last and so on. And usually, at least in enterprises which have long experience and good standing in the field of industrial relations, such rules are either laid down in written agreements or established by practice.

§4. The Issues for Collective Bargaining

214. Although it adopted its unfair labour practices law from American law, Japanese law is different in that it does not, in general, specify issues for bargaining which are compulsory or mandatory. Thus, in Japanese legal theory and in practice a wide range of issues are susceptible to collective bargaining: in fact almost all the issues over which the employer has any control are regarded as coming within the scope of bargaining. The argument of the 'management prerogative' has rarely been accepted – except by management idéologues. The only legislative provision in this area, Art. 8 of the PCNELR Law, excludes matters which affect the management and operation of public corporations and national enterprises from collective bargaining. While this provision does, in any case, apply only to the public sector, it has still been criticised as curtailing the right of the workers to bargain. Furthermore, it has also been criticised on the grounds that in practice many of the matters affecting the management and operation of the enterprise also affect working conditions. For instance, it is often pointed out that the timetabling of the trains on the National Railway is a matter affecting management and operation; but it also inevitably affects the working hours and shifts of the workers and so should not be excluded from bargaining. However, under enterprise unionism, if we pursue this logic everything which concerns the management in a particular enterprise comes within the scope of bargaining since everything will affect the working conditions of the workers in that enterprise. Thus, theoretically, it is generally admitted that the employer has an obligation to bargain about all aspects of managerial decisions if they affect working conditions.

215. Political issues and other problems which are beyond the control of the management either legally or practically are outside the scope of collective bargaining. This point will be important in connection with the legality of strikes – especially political and sympathetic strikes – which will be discussed in Chapter V.

§5. Collective Bargaining and Workers' Consultation

216. The distinction between collective bargaining and workers' consultation has never been very clear in Japanese industrial relations. Workers' consultation (*rōshi kyōgi* in Japanese) is distinguished from collective bargaining only in the terminology of collective agreements where it is regarded as a different method of negotiating for management and labour to use. However, since consultation is introduced by collective agreements between the enterprise union and the employer, (approximately 77 per cent of all agreements surveyed by the Ministry of Labour in 1979), it also takes place between the delegates of the union and the employer. So bargaining and consultation are both carried out by the same union, even though different people may represent the union in each case. The issues to be discussed differ according to the scope of the collective agreements, although they often overlap.

217. In general, collective bargaining will be used to decide about matters such as working conditions; while consultation will be used to deal with problems which are supposed not to be suitable for bargaining – which is, after all, a form of confrontation. This latter category includes dismissal, transfer and promotion, changes in production, sales or other management policies, the introduction of new methods, technology or facilities, the abolition of certain plants or work divisions and so on. Matters which are regarded as matters of managerial prerogative by the management side are certainly not suitable for collective bargaining; especially in Japan where, as we have already mentioned, bargaining tends to be more or less a matter of confrontation (see para. 212).

218. As a result, in enterprises where union–management relations are more mature, they will agree to avoid unnecessary and useless confrontation; settling the matter instead by mutual understanding in the form of consultation. Thus, in industrial relations terms, in most of these mature enterprises consultation is regarded as a peaceful and reasonable attempt to reach an understanding of the problems, whereas bargaining is regarded as a situation of show-down and confrontation in which there can be no discussion but only negotiation. (As a matter of fact, in many collective agreements the issues suitable for bargaining and those suitable for consultation overlap, and the same issue will be a matter for collective bargaining after consultation has failed to settle it. Therefore, it is fairly common in Japan for consultation to be regarded as a preliminary step to collective bargaining.) However, legally speaking, the distinction is not at all clear – or rather the law does not recognise workers' consultation as distinct from bargaining. As far as consultation takes place between the union and the employer the law may regard it as collective bargaining; but at the same time another possible interpretation is that they are legally different since the parties themselves differentiate between them. The theories, the Courts and the Labour Relations Commissions are all confused, sometimes admitting that the employer has met his obligation to bargain if he has consulted with the representatives of the union and sometimes laying down that the employer is liable for refusing to bargain if he has preferred to consult and refused to 'bargain'.

§6. Bargaining in Good Faith

219. The employer's obligation to bargain does not include the obligation to reach an agreement; however it does include the obligation to try in good faith to reach an agreement. Bargaining in good faith requires the employer, among other things, to make counter-proposals, to disclose information and to refrain from negotiating with individual union members. Unlike the present American system, Japanese law does not recognise unfair labour practices on the labour side. This has caused some resentment among the employers who blame the one-sidedness of the law in favour of labour. However, at least the refusal of the union to bargain will be taken into account by the Courts and the

Commissions; they have held that the refusal of the employer to bargain does not amount to an unfair labour practice when the union has taken a rather obstinate or unreasonable attitude or, needless to say, when the union has refused to bargain at all.

§7. The Conclusion of Collective Agreements

220. The Trade Union Law provides that a collective agreement will be effective when it is in the form of a document either signed by or under the hand and seal of both parties. Only parties which are qualified to bargain (as explained above, see §2) can be party to the collective agreement. On the labour side, the union must be a permanent organisation which is capable of respecting the obligations and claiming the rights resulting from the agreement. The formality required by the Trade Union Law is often neglected, the majority view being the unwritten agreements between the union and the management should also be recognised as collective agreements and given the full legal effect of written agreements which have been signed or sealed. As yet the Courts have been rather reluctant to accept this view.

§8. The Term of the Collective Agreement and its Termination

221. The Trade Union Law provides that the maximum length of a collective agreement is three years, and an agreement in which a term of validity exceeding three years is provided for shall still be regarded as one with a three-year term. According to the law, an agreement in which no term of validity is provided for may be terminated by a written notice of termination with either the signature or the name affixed by seal of one of the parties. The period of notice must be at least ninety days. The maximum period of three years is provided by law on the grounds that too long a term of validity will restrict the flexibility of industrial relations. However, the appropriateness of the three-year maximum may be in doubt, considering the recent development of long-term agreements with escalator clauses to meet the continuing inflation. But in Japan today most agreements, especially wage agreements, are still concluded for one year because of the practice of the spring offensive. The law does not mention the possibility of terminating an agreement for a definite period while it is still effective and within the prescribed period. Legal theory and the Courts agree that termination is only possible when the fundamental basis of the agreement has been destroyed; for example, when one of the parties has repeatedly neglected the basis obligations of the agreement.

§9. Legal Effect of the Collective Agreement

I. The Contents of the Collective Agreement

222. Adopting the traditional German theory, the majority of legal theorists divide the contents of the collective agreement into two parts: the normative part with normative effect and the obligatory part with obligatory effect. Some add a third part: the institutional part which has both normative and obligatory effect. Others take a different approach altogether, and divide the provisions of the collective agreement into three parts: the part concerned with individual labour relations, the part concerned with collective labour relations and the part concerned with both individual an collective labour relations. The normative part and the obligatory part in the first theory roughly correspond to the individual part and the collective part in the third theory respectively. The provisions concerning working conditions and the other contents of the individual contract are usually regarded as having normative effect, while the collective part merely establishes mutual obligations between the employer and the union who are the parties to the agreement. According to the second theory, the institutional part corresponds to the third part of the third theory. Institutional provisions are provisions which require consultation with or the permission of the union before a decision to transfer or dismiss union members or to change individual personal status is taken. Union-shop clauses are also regarded as institutional provisions. Such provisions impose some obligations on the employer: to consult with or get the permission of the union before taking certain decisions and to dismiss particular employees at the request of the union; but at the same time, according to the majority theory, they have normative effect in the sense that a dismissal which contradicts these provisions is null and void.

II. Normative Effect

223. The Trade Union Law lays down that any provision in an individual contract which contravenes the standard of working conditions and other treatment provided for workers in a collective agreement shall be null and void; and that the invalidated part of the individual contract shall be replaced by the appropriate provision in the collective agreement. It also lays down that the same rule shall apply to any part of the collective agreement which is not provided for in the individual contract. The normative effect of the collective agreement is regarded as being the most fundamental of its effects, since the main purpose of the collective agreement is certainly to improve the working conditions and the general treatment of the workers at the work place. However, the problem is raised as to whether the provision of better working conditions in the individual contract should be interpreted as 'contravening' the standards of the collective agreement or not. The majority view answers this question in the affirmative. This attitude reflects a trend in the Japanese trade union movement whereby the job of the union is often regarded as controlling the working conditions of the workers rather than simply imposing certain minimum conditions and leaving room for individual development. It is also a characteristic of enterprise unionism that it is the job of the union to *decide* the actual working conditions in each enterprise instead of merely establishing the minimum standard of working conditions in an industry and then allowing higher conditions in individual enterprises.

224. The coverage of the normative effect of a collective agreement is limited to the working conditions of members of the union which is a party to the agreement; although the same working conditions are in fact also provided for any unorganised employees in the enterprise, regardless of the extension of the effect of the collective agreement (see below). When other unions are involved the effect of the agreement is not extended to their members; although sometimes the new conditions are provided for them also if their unions have actually demanded different conditions. In such a case the employer often encounters difficult problems in respect of his obligation to bargain in good faith (as described in §6). However, as far as the legal effect of the collective agreement is concerned, the standpoint of the legal principle is quite clear: it is effective only for members of the union which is a party to the agreement.

225. The normative effect of the collective agreement is recognised not only in connection with the individual contract, but also in connection with the work rules and any other documents and agreements concerning the working conditions and treatment of union members. Only the compulsory legislative and other legal norms are in a position superior to the collective agreement; in other words, the provisions of a collective agreement which contradict the compulsory legal norms are null and void but otherwise the provisions of collective agreements are of almost primary importance in governing individual labour relations.

226. As we have already mentioned, the majority view does not accept the principle of 'favourability' (Günstigkeitprinzip) with regard to the normative effect of collective agreements. In the face of this attitude a rather influential minority view has been emerging to support the principle, claiming that the improved conditions – whether gained by individual bargaining or brought in voluntarily by the employer – should not be denied of their legality just because a collective agreement has provided for a lower standard. According to this view it is absurd to give in to the union pressure for inferior conditions for workers who are better than average. While the majority of theorists still assert that favourable treatment for certain individual workers is harmful to the influence of the union and should be denied legal effect, the minority view is that favourable treatment should be denied legal effect only when it is being used by the employer to interfere with the influence of the union.

III. Obligatory Effect

227. All the provisions of a collective agreement have an obligatory effect in the sense that the collective agreement is an agreement between private parties and as such has the same effect as an ordinary contract, giving rights and obligations respectively to both of the parties to the contract. However, the provisions dealing with individual labour relations also have normative effect, as we have seen, and the employer has an obligation to the union to observe these provisions and to provide conditions for its members which are in accordance with them. This obligation is called an 'obligation of execution' (Durchführungspflicht).

228. Otherwise, provisions which set up rights and obligations between the employer and the union which is party to the agreement have the same effect as an ordinary contract in civil law. The obligatory effects are, however, usually meaningful only in theory and not in practice. This is because most of the obligations imposed by collective agreements are not really suitable for enforcement through civil law procedure. For instance, the obligation to bargain or consult with the union is not very easy to enforce using the civil law. The most important effect might be the damage caused by the non-observance of the provisions, but here again damage because of the non-observance of an obligation to bargain or consult does not make very much sense. On the other hand, the union's obligations are rather suitable for indemnity. For example, the damage caused by a strike held in breach of a no-strike clause is rather easy for the employer to recover. Thus, theoretically, the obligatory effect of the collective agreement is more inclined to protect the employer's interests. However, the unions have been trying to take advantage of the obligatory effect of collective agreements by asking the Courts to issue temporary orders or injunctions to force the employers to observe the provisions of their collective agreements. Although some of the obligations are not enforceable by law the unions can put pressure on the employer with these temporary orders and injunctions, even though they might not be enforceable in the final analysis if the employer challenged them definitely in Court.

229. An 'obligation of execution' may be regarded as just one of the obligatory effects of a collective agreement. But its importance is emphasised by the fact that it enables the union to request the Court to issue a temporary order or decision declaring the existence of the employer's obligation to provide the working conditions laid down in the collective agreement. The union does not need to get the agreement of all its members in order for it to be able to assert their rights deriving from the collective agreement before the Court. The union can sue the employer in its own name without the agreement of individual members.

IV. The So-Called 'Institutional' Effect

230. The provisions concerning both individual and collective labour relations undoubtedly have the effect of establishing rights and obligations between the parties to the agreement. Some problems arise with regard to the normative effect of such provisions. It is, however, generally agreed that provisions which ask that the employer bargains, consults or gets the permission of the union in respect of the dismissal, transfer or disciplinary punishment of union members have normative effect. This means that dismissals or other legal action taken without the requisite obligations having been fulfilled are regarded as null and void – although opinions are divided about the effect of the union-shop and other union security clauses. In this case we shall restrict our discussion mainly to the effect of the union-shop clause, since it is almost the only union security clause actually used in Japan.

231. The normative effect of the union-shop clause has been widely accepted, which means that the effect of a dismissal requested by a union and based on a union-shop clause depends on the effectiveness of the union-shop clause and also on the effectiveness of the union's decision to expel the member from the union. If the union-shop clause is illegal or ineffective for any reason, or if the reason for the expulsion of the member is illegal or ineffective, then according to this widely-held view the dismissal is null and void. As a result of this argument, it is generally accepted that a dismissal is legal if an effective union-shop clause exists and if the union's request for dismissal is based on a legal expulsion or some other well-founded reason such as a refusal to join the union or a withdrawal from the union. There is a minority body of opinion which challenges this contention; arguing instead that the effectiveness of the dismissal should be judged according to whether the employer is entitled by the work rules, the individual contract or some other legal rule to take such action. In the opinion of the minority, the view of the majority of theorists is that the employer's right to dismiss can be extended by a union-shop clause without any other legal foundation. This is against the 'Günstigkeitsprinzip'. Thus, the difference between the majority and minority theories at this point depends on whether they accept the above principle or not. The minority group also argues that it is absurd to make the effectiveness of the dismissal dependent on the effectiveness of the union's decision, which the employer has nothing to do with.

V. The Peace Obligation

232. The majority view is that the parties to a collective agreement have an obligation which is inherent in its very nature to refrain from engaging in acts of dispute – including strikes and lock-outs – aimed at challenging the contents of the agreement during its term of effectiveness. This obligation, still according to the majority view, cannot be denied even with the agreement of both parties since it is inherent in the collective agreement. However, it is relative in the sense that acts of dispute are prohibited only during the effective term of the agreement, and even then only acts of dispute which challenge the contents of the agreement. Otherwise, acts of dispute are permitted, both after the termination of the agreement and even during the effective term of the agreement if the act of dispute is over an issue not mentioned in the agreement. Of course, in an actual industrial relations situation it is often open to question whether a certain issue is laid down in the agreement or not. For instance, when the exact amount of wages is laid down in the agreement does this mean that it excludes the possibility of an extra bonus? The Courts have tried to interpret the meaning of provisions of collective agreements in more or less the same way as they interpret contracts in general; seeking to discover the intentions of the parties through various means such as taking into account the customs and practices in use, considering the bargaining situation which resulted in the agreement and so on. In fact they often find it very difficult to discover the real intentions of the parties, since the parties sometimes leave the provisions vague quite intentionally – expecting the rather flexibile development of industrial relations which depends on a mutual understanding of the Japanese way. As a result, in Japan, strikes are rarely found to be in breach of the peace obligation; in spite of the employers' repeated challenges in the Courts.

233. Since the peace obligation inherent in the collective agreement is only of a relative nature some parties have tried to extend it to cover all acts of dispute during the effective term of the agreement. The so-called 'absolute' peace obligation, established by a provision in the agreement to prohibit every act of dispute regardless of its aim, is effective – at least according to the majority view. The minority view is rather that such provisions contradict the constitutional guarantee of the right to strike. However, the majority of theorists asserts that the right to strike can be surrendered, especially when it is only during the term of effectiveness of the agreement.

VI. Extension of the Effect of a Collective Agreement

234. The Trade Union Law provides for two kinds of extension of the effect of collective agreements. One is the general binding force in the plant and the other is that in the locality. The first is recognised automatically when three-quarters of the employees of a similar kind in a plant or work place come under the application of a collective agreement and the effect of the agreement is extended to cover the rest of the employees of a similar kind in the plant or work place. The second is recognised by the decision of the Labour Minister or the Governor of the prefecture to extend the effect of an agreement which applies to the majority of similar workers in a certain locality to the remaining workers of the same kind in the same locality and their employers. The decision of the Labour Minister or the Governor is taken at the request of one or both of the parties to the collective agreement which is to be extended, and in accordance with the resolution of the Labour Relations Commission. The Commission may amend any of the provisions in the agreement which it finds inappropriate before making the resolution to extend. As we have already mentioned, the right to bargain collectively is guaranteed to minority unions too. Thus, the extension of the effect of an agreement is interpreted as not covering the members of those unions which have their own agreements.

235. There is no doubt that the extension of the effect of an agreement is recognised only with regard to provisions governing the working conditions and treatment of employees. Provisions which cover the obligations between the employer and the union are not of an extendible nature.

VII. The Effect of a Collective Agreement after its Termination

236. Contrary to German law, Japanese law does not have anything to say about the effect of a collective agreement after its termination. The Trade Union Law provides that the parties may include a provision stating that the agreement is to remain in effect for an indefinite period after the expiry of its original term until a new agreement is concluded. Such a provision is called an 'automatic extension clause'. Some agreements also include provisions to the effect that the same agreement with the same contents will be renewed if a new agreement has not been concluded before it expires. This is called an 'automatic renewal clause'. Through such provisions the parties can avoid the so-called 'vacant' period when there is no collective agreement. However, if the parties have not made any such arrangement and the agreement has become ineffective because it has expired or for some other reason, how are working conditions to be decided? This is a more or less theoretical question since in most cases the same working conditions are laid down in the work rules; and even if they are not the parties will usually follow the pattern of the past. The real question is whether one of the parties can change the existing conditions without the consent of the other, and this question has been discussed in terms of the so-called 'after-effect' (Nachwirkung) of the collective agreement. Leading theorists tend to deny this effect of the collective agreement, saying that the standard of working conditions already laid down may not be changed without both parties' agreement since these conditions have been integrated into the *individual* contracts of the workers who are union members during the term of effectiveness of the agreement and cannot, therefore, be changed without the consent of both parties to the *individual* contract.

237. So, according to the majority view, the contents of a collective agreement remain effective after its termination merely as the contents of individual contracts. The working conditions specified by the former collective agreement will remain binding on the employer and on the workers who are union members only until new collective agreements or new individual contracts have been drawn up. In other words, the 'after-effect' of the collective agreement is recognised and explained by the majority only in terms of its effect on individual contracts. The minority view, however, is that even after termination the contents of a collective agreement cannot be altered until a new collective agreement has been concluded. But this brings about the rather absurd result that the employer can never enforce lower working conditions for the unions will never agree to them. Whatever the case, the 'after effect' of the collective agreement is recognised only with regard to those provisions which concern individual labour relations.

Chapter V. Acts of Dispute

§1. The Notion of Acts of Dispute

238. The Constitution guarantees the 'right to act collectively' for all workers. Both in actual industrial relations and in labour law theory the term 'act of dispute' is frequently used to mean a variety of union actions for strike purposes. The Labour Relations Adjustment Law gives the following definitions of 'labour dispute' and 'act of dispute'. 'Labour dispute' means 'a disagreement over claims arising between the parties concerned with labour relations regarding labour relations and resulting in either the occurrence of an act of dispute or in conditions where there is the danger of an act of dispute occurring' (Art. 6 of the Labour Relations Adjustment Law). 'Act of dispute' means 'strikes, go-slows, lock-outs and other acts and counter-acts hampering the normal course of work in an enterprise and performed by the parties concerned with labour relations with the object of attaining their respective claims' (Art. 7 of the same law).

239. Although these definitions are given in order to specify the necessary conditions for the initiation of the dispute settlement procedures provided by the Labour Relations Adjustment Law, they are also relied on for the interpretation of the law which deals with the legal effect of acts of dispute. Through the constitutional guarantee of the right to act collectively and the rather broad definition of an act of dispute in the labour Relations Adjustment Law there is a remarkable tendency in Japanese industrial relations to admit the legality of a variety of actions taken by the unions which hamper the normal course of business. Also, because the constitutional guarantee of the right to act collectively only applies to workers, the employer's right to lock-out suffers badly from being very extensively restricted – especially when compared with the extensive legal recognition granted to acts of dispute by the unions.

§2. Proper Acts of Dispute

240. As a result of the constitutional guarantee of the right to act collectively, a legal indemnity (exemption from legal liability) is recognised – both in civil and in crininal law – for trade union activities. In order to be given indemnity the act must be carried out by a trade union and must be of a proper kind and have a lawful purpose.

I. Acts by Bona Fide Unions

241. The act should be carried out by a bona fide union. For their acts of dispute to be protected unions need not be registered or qualified under the Trade Union Law (see Part II, Chapter 1, §1); although they do have to be bona fide unions. Workers' organisations which confine themselves principally to backing political or social movements, to providing mutual aid, or doing other welfare work are not entitled to indemnity. The workers' group which is not organised in the sense of having its own rules and representatives is not granted legal indemnity for its actions either. The same is true of a group within a union which engages in acts of dispute without official authorisation from the union (unauthorised or wild-cat strikes). However, some theorists contend that an *ad hoc* workers' organisation established for the purpose of a strike should also be granted indemnity in so far as it has representatives with whom the employer can negotiate and who will be responsible for the settlement of the dispute.

II. The Purpose of the Act of Dispute

242. With regard to the purpose of acts of dispute, the theorists are split. The more orthodox theories and majority of legal decisions confine indemnity to those actions taken for the purpose of getting better working conditions by means of bargaining with the employer. They claim that a proper act of dispute must have an 'economic' purpose and that such acts done for 'political' purposes are not to be given indemnity. According to them, the 'sympathetic' strike which is called for the purpose of helping another union which is involved in a dispute tends to be improper because the employer of members of a union which is engaging in a sympathetic strike has no authority to settle the original dispute and is not even in a position to negotiate about the disputed issues. They regard the act of dispute as a means of negotiating, and recognise its legality only in so far as it is used to increase the bargaining strength of the union. Other theorists, opposing this view, regard the right to act collectively as being independent of the right to bargain; and insist that the Constitution has legalised every action of the union, regardless of its purpose, if the action itself is proper. Thus, according to this latter view, the political or sympathetic strike is also legal. However, since the civil indemnity means that the employer cannot claim reparation for damage caused by the act of dispute, it is not very fair to allow it in a case where the employer has no authority to settle the dispute because it concerns a matter in another company or a political issue.

III. Proper Acts of Dispute

243. Art. 1, Sec. 2 of the Trade Union Law declares that in no event shall acts of violence be construed as appropriate acts for trade unions. Needless to say, not only violence but also threats, coercion, defamation and injury, not to mention homicide and similar criminal acts, are not permitted even as acts of dispute. On the other hand, as we have already noted, the same article of the Trade Union Law lays down a criminal indemnity. This superficial contradiction is generally solved by interpreting it to mean that there is criminal indemnity for those criminal acts which would possibly amount to threats, coercion or trespass in ordinary civil life but which are usually accepted by trade unionists as ordinary acts in the course of industrial relations when they are demanding to negotiate, trying to persuade strike-breakers and so on. In any case, the law allows criminal and civil indemnity for 'acts of dispute', a phrase which is regarded as including a variety of acts and not just strikes or go-slows. Thus, what is a proper act of dispute should be considered separately for each category of act which is regularly used in Japanese industrial relations.

§3. Different Types of Acts of Dispute

I. Strikes

244. Japan is one of those countries where the unions have invented a variety of acts of dispute with which to embarrass the management. Not only is the strike just one of the many types of industrial action which are normally used, it is not even the most typical or the most representative of all the acts of dispute used in Japanese industrial relations.

245. International strike statistics do not reflect the real situation very accurately because the Japanese official strike statistics include those strikes which lasted for more than 4 hours but do not include acts of dispute other than strikes and lock-outs. In the statistics given in Table XXVII for other countries strikes, go-slows and lock-outs which lasted for more than 8 hours are counted. If we take into consideration the fact that there are so many acts of dispute other than strike in Japan, we may presume that the frequency of acts of dispute in Japan is higher than these statistics actually show.

246. The short duration of strikes is one of the characteristics of Japanese industrial relations; in fact one hour or two hour strikes are very common and the majority of strikes continue for one or two days at the most, so a strike which lasts for a week will be regarded as a very long strike. The short duration of Japanese strikes is probably best understood if we consider the actual function of the strike in Japan and remember the existence of various other acts of dispute. For in Japan the strike is not the final weapon in collective bargaining. Often there will be a strike before any bargaining has even taken place, and so quite naturally the unions may stop the strike and the members go back to work without the dispute having actually been settled. During any dispute there may be a series of strikes, and this can be explained by the fact that strikes in Japan are designed to attract the employer's attention. As a matter of fact, a strike is regarded as a demonstration of feeling rather than as a weapon with which to press the management after negotiations have reached deadlock. Therefore, the act of dispute need not be something which causes serious economic damage, like a long-standing strike: a minor irritating embarrassment will do instead. This is the reason why in Japan there are so many different acts of dispute, which as we are about to see take all kinds of imaginable forms.

247. A strike is regarded as a proper type of act of dispute unless its purpose,

TABLE XXVII

Labour Disputes in the Major Countries

	Japan				USA				UK			
Year	Number of Disputes	Working Days Lost (in thousands)	Working Days Lost per 10 Employed Workers	Duration (Days)	Number of Disputes	Working Days Lost (in thousands)	Working Days Lost per 10 Employed Workers	Duration (Days)	Number of Disputes	Working Days Lost (in thousands)	Working Days Lost per 10 Employed Workers	Duration (Days)
1965	1,542	5,669	2.0	3.4	3,963	23,300	3.8	15.0	2,354	2,925	1.2	3.3
67	1,214	1,830	0.6	2.5	4,595	42,100	6.4	14.7	2,116	2,787	1.2	3.8
68	1,546	2,841	0.9	2.4	5,045	49,018	7.2	18.5	2,378	4,690	2.0	2.1
69	1,783	3,634	1.1	2.6	5,700	42,869	6.1	18.6	3,116	6,846	3.0	4.1
70	2,260	3,915	1.2	2.3	5,716	66,414	9.4	20.1	3,906	10,980	4.8	6.1
71	2,527	6,029	1.8	3.2	5,318	47,589	6.7	14.5	2,228	13,551	6.1	11.5
72	2,498	5,147	1.5	3.3	5,010	27,066	3.7	15.8	2,497	23,910	11.0	13.8
73	3,326	4,604	1.3	2.1	5,353	27,950	3.6	12.4	2,873	7,200	3.3	4.7
74	5,211	9,663	2.7	2.7	5,074	47,991	6.1	17.3	2,922	14,750	6.6	9.0
75	3,391	8,016	2.2	2.9	5,031	31,240	4.1	17.9	2,282	6,010	2.7	7.4
76	2,720	3,254	0.9	2.4	5,648	23,962	3.0	15.8	2,016	3,284	1.5	5.0
77	1,712	1,518	0.4	2.2	5,506	21,258	2.6	17.5	2,703	10,142	4.7	8.8
78	1,517	1,358	0.4	2.1	4,230	23,774	2.7	23.6	2,471	9,405	4.1	9.4
79	1,153	930	0.2	2.1	4,827	20,409	2.3	20.0	2,080	29,474	12.9	6.2
80	1,133	1,001	0.3	1.8	3,885	20,844	2.3	26.2	1,330	11,964	5.4	14.3
81	955	554	0.1	2.2	2,577	16,908	1.9	23.2	1,338	4,266	2.0	2.8
82	944	538	0.1	2.5	—	9,061	1.0	13.8	1,528	5,313	2.5	2.5

	W. Germany				France				Italy			
Year	Number of Disputes	Working Days Lost (in thousands)	Working Days Lost per 10 Employed Workers	Duration (Days)	Number of Disputes	Working Days Lost (in thousands)	Working Days Lost per 10 Employed Workers	Duration (Days)	Number of Disputes	Working Days Lost (in thousands)	Working Days Lost per 10 Employed Workers	Duration (Days)
1965	20	49	0.0	8.2	1,674	980	0.7	1.4	3,191	6,993	7.9	3.0
67	742	390	0.2	6.5	1,675	4,204	2.8	1.5	2,658	8,568	9.5	3.8
68	36	25	0.0	1.2	1,103	423	0.3	0.9	3,377	9,240	10.2	1.9
69	86	249	0.1	2.8	2,480	2,224	1.4	1.5	3,788	37,825	41.2	5.0
70	129	93	0.0	0.5	3,319	1,742	1.1	1.5	4,162	20,887	22.3	5.6
71	624	4,484	2.0	7.8	4,358	4,388	2.7	1.4	5,598	14,799	15.7	3.8
72	53	66	0.0	3.0	3,464	3,760	2.3	1.4	4,765	19,497	20.0	4.4
73	732	563	0.3	3.0	3,731	3,910	2.4	1.6	3,769	23,402	15.0	3.8
74	890	1,051	0.5	4.2	3,381	3,380	1.9	2.2	5,174	19,467	12.1	2.5
75	202	70	0.2	1.9	3,876	3,876	2.2	2.1	3,601	25,189	16.7	1.9
76	1,481	534	0.2	3.1	4,348	5,011	2.8	1.1	2,706	25,378	15.4	2.1
77	81	24	0.0	0.6	3,302	3,666	2.0	1.9	3,308	16,566	9.9	1.2
78	1,239	4,281	1.9	8.8	3,206	2,200	1.2	3.1	2,479	10,177	6.0	1.2
79	40	483	0.2	6.2	3,104	3,637	2.0	3.8	2,000	27,530	15.9	1.7
80	132	128	0.1	2.8	3,542	1,674	0.9	3.3	2,238	16,457	9.3	1.2
81	297	58	0.0	0.2	2,504	1,496	0.8	4.5	2,204	10,527	5.9	1.3
82	40	15	0.0	0.4	3,240	2,327	–	5.0	–	–	–	–

Source: Japan Productivity Centre *Practical Statistics 1977–1984*

or the nature of the body organising it, or some of the acts accompanying it – such as picketing or sit-downs – cause problems. A partial strike, which means that some of the union members go on strike while others continue working, is also quite legal in Japan; although some difficult problems do arise with regard to the wages of those who continued to work (see Chapter V §4 IV).

II. Going-Slow (Soldiering), Working-To-Rule etc.

248. Going-slow (soldiering) and working-to-rule are both methods which are commonly used in the Japanese industrial relations situation; partly because of the nature of industrial action as a demonstration and partly because of the comparatively poor financial position of the unions.

249. At the same time this type of act of dispute is frequently resorted to in the public sector where the law prohibits acts of dispute. The unions claim that they are not engaging in an act of dispute by taking such an obscure type of action. Especially when working-to-rule, the unions claim that they are only observing the law or the work rules and are not disturbing business. However, these acts are regarded as acts of dispute in so far as they actually disturb the every day running of the business; even if they do not disrupt business in a strict legal way. They are not regarded as illegal as such, since the workers are merely refusing to provide a part of their work while in a strike they refuse to provide the whole of it – so according to this logic they are causing less harm. But even these acts of dispute can cause problems, particularly with regard to the wages of those who are partially refusing to work.

250. Furthermore, such acts of dispute should be regarded as improper and illegal if they are in any way malicious. For instance, while going-slow is not of itself improper, if it is done in a service industry by those who work directly with the customers working very slowly and irritating them it will be regarded as sabotage rather than as simply going-slow and will therefore be improper.

III. Taking Holidays

251. The unions may order all or most of their members to take their annual holiday on the same day, which will have the same effect as them going on strike. This type of act of dispute was originally started, and has often been resorted to since, in the public sector where acts of dispute are prohibited. The unions are able to claim that they are not engaging in an act of dispute but are only taking legally recognised holidays. Unions in the private sector have also resorted to this kind of act of dispute sometimes, especially when they have felt that a normal strike would be financially difficult. So, this is a peculiar kind of act of dispute during which union members continue to claim wages.

252. But the Courts, as well as most of the theories, have held that this is indeed a kind of act of dispute since it is undertaken for the purpose of disturbing the normal course of business in order to assert the union's demands against the management, and such wage claims have therefore been denied. However, a difficult problem arises when we consider the legal effect of a worker taking a holiday on the orders of the union and then participating in some union activity at a work place other than his own. In this case some Court decisions – including a Supreme Court decision – and some of the theories say that the act of taking a holiday does not disturb the normal course of business in *the worker's own work place* (even though he might have disturbed business in the other work place) and that such an act should be regarded simply as engaging in union activity while on holiday, like attending a union meeting. From this point of view there is no reason why the worker's wage claim should not succeed.

IV. Pasting Posters, Wearing Ribbons etc.

253. Pasting posters on the walls and windows of the company premises and wearing ribbons, arm-bands or head-bands with the union's demands or other slogans written on them are all actions which are quite frequently resorted to during labour disputes. Of course such activities were originally a source of propaganda for the union and a means of communicating information to the union members, non-union workers, customers and the general public about the position of the union and the situation which gave rise to the dispute. However, in Japanese industrial relations today this type of action is mainly taken with the intention of disturbing the normal course of business or embarassing the management, rather than for purposes of communication. The unions paste an enormous number – often hundreds and sometimes thousands – of rather shabby and poorly-made posters in a disorderly fashion on the elegant company buildings, with bucketfuls of paste pouring down the walls and windows. In many cases the company will need to employ special workers to clean the building, because the posters are often put back repeatedly as soon as they have been taken away and the excess paste is left all over the walls. The wearing of arm-bands, head-bands or ribbons disturbs the normal course of business when the appearance of the employees is important – especially in the service industries. This is also the case with regard to the clothing of production workers – their appearance is often regulated by work-rules for reasons of safety. These acts are not necessarily improper (and, therefore, illegal) because acts to hamper the normal course of business are allowed as acts of dispute; and so only the most extreme acts, which are felt to be unfair or abusive, will be deemed to be improper and illegal.

254. Judgments differ according to individual circumstances and it is hard to generalise. For instance, the Courts and the Labour Relations Commissions are split about the legality of workers in hotels wearing ribbons with the union's demands written on them. As regards the legality of pasting posters, the Courts usually take into account the degree of excessiveness; namely, the number of posters, their quality and the method of pasting them. It has been held in some cases that pasting posters over and over again, so making the building very dirty and extremely hard to clean, amounts to the crime of destroying the building.

V. Picketing and Sit-Downs

255. Picketing is quite frequently resorted to, either in order to interrupt unorganised employees or to prevent customers entering the company's premises. A sit-down is only another form of picketing, since picketing in Japanese industrial relations means more or less shutting down the flow of traffic through the gates. Quite a number of union members, and often workers from other unions as well, will form ranks in front of the gates standing arm in arm. The predominant theory and some of the Court decisions admit the properness of picketing or sit-downs on the company's premises as long as the union members do not engage in violence. The justification for such illegality they find in the constitutional guarantee of the right to act collectively, which means more than the simple freedom to refuse to work and freedom of speech which together are the sole legal grounds for picketing in the Anglo–American countries.

256. A sit-down is regarded as illegal only when it seriously disturbs the business which is being run by unorganised employees during a strike; either because those sitting down actually disturb the work of others or because they occupy the premises and close the entrance.

VI. Control of the Means of Production or of Management itself

257. In order to achieve the same effect as a picket or a sit-down the unions sometimes take away certain things which belong to the company – such as the means of production – and keep them until the dispute has been settled. The most frequent example of this kind of act is the action taken by the unions in the taxi industry, whereby they take the keys, the car licences or the tyres and hide them somewhere. Another possibility is for the union to keep the money collected by its members from the company's customers for the company and to deposit it in the bank in the union's name until the end of the dispute. Court decisions are divided about the legality of such acts. The reasoning behind those decisions which support their legality is that the unions do not intend to take the goods or the money for ever, but only for the time being; and thus it does not amount to, for example, the crime of embezzlement.

258. Although the legality of even such acts as these is rather dubious, the unions used to resort to much more drastic action – such as taking over the entire management of the company. This kind of act of dispute, called *Seisankari* (production control) in Japanese, was frequently used after the 2nd World War but is not used very often today. One situation in which it may still be used is when the company is going bankrupt; then the unions will occupy the plant and continue the business by themselves. While the Courts deny the legality of such acts, some theorists support them. Furthermore, in practice these acts may well prove effective, since even if they are illegal the employer still has to appeal to the Court to remove the union members and this is often too much trouble for a company on the verge of bankruptcy. Meanwhile the union may make some money or find a solution to the problem.

§4. Legal Effect of the Act of Dispute

I. Civil Indemnity

259. Art. 8 of the Trade Union Law provides that 'no employer shall claim indemnity from a trade union or its members for the damage caused by strikes or other acts of dispute which are proper'. Although this provision only mentions the exemption from liability as against the employer, the theory also holds that because of the constitutional guarantee of the right to act collectively the legal indemnity of the union and its members applies to everybody affected by the act of dispute; and this usually means the customers of the enterprise. Thus, any damage caused by the lawful act of dispute is recoverable only if the customer claims for it against the employer. With the exception of a few theorists, it is generally accepted that the employer is liable to the customers for such damage if he was forced to breach the contract by an act of dispute. As an employer he is responsible for the acts of his employees. The minority view is that the act of dispute should be regarded as an act of God since it is legally guaranteed and the employer cannot help it. Against this, the majority claim that the act of dispute could have been avoided if the employer had tried hard enough; and anyway he must bear even more responsibility for his employees' acts if they are legal.

260. The exemption from civil liability is so comprehensive that it includes breach of contract by individual union members. In other words, union members have no responsibility at all as regards breach of contract, even if they engage in acts of dispute without giving notice, and they are free not only from the responsibility to pay damages but also from any responsibility in connection with the reason for their dismissal. In this sense they are completely exempted from any contractual responsibility whatsoever. The exemption also includes the liability of the union, as well as of the union leaders, in terms of tort. They are completely free from any responsibility for the damage caused by the act of dispute in so far as it is proper in the sense described above.

261. Such a broad exemption from legal liability, covering the union members as well as their leaders, causes difficult problems as to who will be responsible, and to what degree, if the act of dispute turns out to be illegal. This always serves as a reminder of the problem of collective and individual responsibility for the acts of a state which has lost a war. Since individuals are required to give unquestioning obedience to the orders of the state or their superiors during a war, are the same individuals to be prosecuted after the war as war criminals who were responsible for their acts? The international recognition of the responsibility of war criminals seems to be not very popular in Japanese labour law theory. The leading theory tends to deny the responsibility of the members, and sometimes even that of the leaders, claiming that responsibility for an act of dispute should be attributed solely to the union or at the most only to the active leaders. This argument is based on the premises that one cannot expect the rank and file to judge the legality of an act and that those leaders who were against an act cannot be held responsible for it.

II. Criminal Indemnity

262. Art. 1, sect. 2 of the Trade Union Law states that 'the provisions of Article 35 of the Criminal Code shall apply to collective bargaining and other acts of trade unions which are appropriate'. Article 35 of the Criminal Code establishes the legality of acts which are done with the authorisation of the law or as a legitimate business activity even though these acts may, per se, constitute a certain type of crime; for example, the execution of a convicted criminal is not regarded as murder or homicide and an operation by a qualified surgeon never constitutes the crime of injury or violence. Thus, the proper acts of trade unions are regarded as legally authorised acts even if they actually constitute a certain type of crime. However, the real meaning and scope of application of this provision is rather confusing, since it is questionable what kind of crime could ever be called 'appropriate'. A proviso in Art. 1, sect. 2 states that 'in no event shall acts of violence be construed as appropriate acts of trade unions'. In fact the majority theory contends that crimes which involve serious violence cannot be justified; but that otherwise, lighter crimes can be legally authorised. Of course such an assertion is not very convincing in the face of the precise legal provisions justifying certain criminal activities. A compromise interpretation might be as follows: some of the less serious criminal acts which are certainly punishable if they are committed in ordinary circumstances by ordinary citizens may be justified if they are done in the process of collective bargaining or during an act of dispute. A typical case might be when trade unionists enter the offices of the management shouting, threatening and demanding to bargain, successfully force a meeting and eventually refuse to leave in spite of management requests to do so. In such cases, as long as their attitude was not too violent or excessively threatening, they will not be punished for crimes such as threatening behaviour, coercion or trespass.

III. Legal Effect of an Act of Dispute on the Union Movement

263. The description which we have given of the legality of acts of dispute in Japan might sound much too tolerant and rather absurd to Western readers. Only a few theorists have voiced any doubts about the wisdom of such broad legality for trade union acts. Even a number of judges have agreed that acts of dispute can include something more positive than the mere passive refusal to work and have justified actual physical force – which is often carefully, but never very convincingly, distinguished from the prohibited 'violence'. Such attitudes stem from the desire of the judges and the legal theorists to support the trade union cause; which, as they see it, needs protection against the tyrannical employers. However, it can hardly be denied that it is possible that such a 'protective' attitude on the part of the lawyers may have spoilt the unions' sincere drive to become more powerful organisations in terms of solidarity and finance, and instead they continue to place too much reliance on the 'powerful' confrontation at the bargaining or dispute stage.

IV. Acts of Dispute and Wages

264. Because of the legal nature of the act of dispute in Japan all acts of dispute are conducted without terminating the employment contract. In spite of the continuance of the contract it is agreed in principle that union members will not receive their wages during a strike. Of course difficult problems often arise with regard to the amount of wages lost during a strike; and there are still more problems to consider in the case of other acts of dispute, when the union members have actually come to the work place and eventually done at least part of their work. Taking the case of a full-scale strike first, the unions have challenged the legality of the employers' practice of deducting wages according to the number of days lost during the strike; that is, the system of wage deduction whereby one twenty-fifth of the total monthly wage will be deducted if the union goes on strike for one day out of the 25 working days in a month. The unions claimed that it was unlawful for the whole amount of wages for the days on strike to be deducted because some part of the wages should be retained in proportion to the days off: for instance, if the employee was sick for a few days this would include parts of the wages such as the family allowance and the housing allowance. Some judges have in fact accepted this argument. The reasoning behind such decisions is that there are certain parts of the wages which are not directly connected with the daily work, and as such should not be deducted just because the employee did not work on a certain day – regardless of the reason for his absence, strike or sickness. However, it is not very easy in practice to distinguish between those parts of the wages which are connected with daily work and those parts which are not. An example would be allowances such as extra payments to the head of a section, which may be either for his work or for his position. The minority view is that the whole of the wages are paid for the employee's work regardless of the name of various allowances and that therefore the whole amount should be deducted.

265. In the case of partial strikes and other acts of dispute in which all or part of the union membership comes to work and eventually does at least part of the work expected of it the problem of how much the employer should pay is a fairly pressing one. During a partial strike ordered by the union even those members who come to work cannot be as effective as usual and so, theoretically speaking, the employer may deduct part of the wages of those who attended and need not pay anything to those who were absent altogether. If in the course of an act of dispute they only do a part of their normal work, then the employer may also deduct a certain amount from their wages. However, it is at least questionable whether the employer may deduct from the wages in accordance with the decreased production on a particular day in comparison with the average production per day under normal circumstances. The union may be able to argue that the reduction on that day was not caused by their action alone but that other factors were involved, or even that in certain industries – and perhaps in offices – it is impossible to expect an average performance each day because peculiar conditions will arise almost every day which cannot be predicted. No legal decision has yet been reached on this point, and opinions are divided. Of course the employer may lock the union members out and refuse to pay them their full wages – both in the event of a partial strike and during other acts of dispute (see the next paragraph).

V. Lock-Outs

266. Whether the employers' right to lock-out is recognised or not is a real problem in Japan, as the Constitution guarantees the right to act collectively only to workers. The majority of theorists admit the right of employers to lock workers out for 'balance' or 'fairness' between employer and worker; but a minority do not agree with this rather ambiguous reasoning and, basing their argument on civil law principles, maintain that employers can refuse to pay wages when the workers are not providing work in accordance with the contract. Also, the majority tend to allow lock-outs only within certain limits. Indeed some theories restrict lawful lock-outs to when the employer is 'defending'; that is, when the union is engaging in some act of dispute. Despite all this the actual results of both theories are not really very different and any discrepancy is mostly in the method of approach.

267. The legal effects of a lock-out are not just limited to wage claims, but also involve the possibility of the expulsion of workers from the company's premises. The question is whether the employer can actually turn out workers who are sitting-in on the premises, and the answer is in the affirmative; but it is rather unnecessary to regard it as having the effect of a lock-out since in any case the employer has the legal right, based on his property rights, to expel anyone who enters and stays on the company premises against his will. The majority of theorists do not recognise the employer's property rights, and therefore have to explain the same legal effect on the basis of his right to lock-out. Anyhow, there is no doubt that the employer may expel workers only after he has gone through the procedures of the Courts; having gained an injunction from the Court he may then enforce it.

§5. Restriction and Prohibition of Acts of Dispute

I. Prohibition of Acts of Dispute which Endanger Human Life

268. The Labour Relations Adjustment Law in Art. 36 prohibits 'any act which hampers or causes a stoppage in the maintenance or normal operation of safety procedures in factories, mines and other places of employment'. This is interpreted as meaning that the law prohibits any act which endangers human life in the work place but not those acts which merely destroy the property of the company. The latter are also regarded as being illegal if they take the form of positive destruction, although they are not prohibited by Art. 36. Negative acts which may eventually cause the destruction of the property (such as refusing to do maintenance work) are not necessarily illegal because in such cases the employer can and may take the steps required to avoid destruction as long as the unions do not obstruct him.

II. Restriction of Acts of Dispute in Public Welfare Work

269. Art. 37 of the Labour Relations Adjustment Law requires the parties concerned in a case involving public welfare work to give notice of any act of dispute to the Labour Relations Commission and the Ministry of Labour or the Prefectural Governor at least 10 days before the day on which the act of dispute is scheduled to begin. Public welfare work is defined by Art. 8 of the same law as work which provides services essential to the daily life of the general public: transportation, post and telecommunications, the supply of water, gas or electricity, medical treatment, public health work and any other work designated by the Prime Minister with the approval of the Diet as work which if stopped for a period of less than one year would seriously affect the national economy or endanger the daily life of the general public. The employer, his organisation, the unions or any other person who is responsible for an act of dispute without giving 10 days' notice will face a maximum fine of one hundred thousand yen.

III. Emergency Adjustment and Acts of Dispute

270. The Prime Minister may decide on an emergency adjustment when he deems that a stoppage, whether because it is in public welfare work or because of the scale of the dispute or the special nature of the work, would pose a serious threat to the national economy or the daily life of the nation. The Prime Minister must ask the opinion of the Central Labour Relations Commission or the Seamen's Central Labour Relations Commission before he makes his decision; and when he has decided he will publish his decision – with his reasons – and notify the Commission of it. After the publication of a decision to make an emergency adjustment the parties are forbidden to engage in any act of dispute for 50 days from the day of publication. The Commission will try to settle the dispute within these 50 days (see Chapter VII). The fine for violating the prohibition cannot exceed two hundred thousand yen.

IV. Prohibition of Acts of Dispute in the Public Sector

271. In the public sector any act which hampers the normal course of operations in a public corporation, a Government enterprise or the public service of the Government is completely prohibited. This prohibition of acts of dispute in the public sector is extremely strict and very broad in two senses. Firstly, all kinds of acts of dispute, including those which are small-scale and fairly harmless, are prohibited if they hamper the normal course of operations in the public sector. Secondly, it covers the whole range of major public corporations and Government enterprises (including such bodies as the Tobacco Monopoly or the National Forests) and all categories of public employees (including simple clerks and even janitors in so far as they are employed by the Government or a public corporation).

272. Such a rigorous prohibition of acts of dispute in the public sector has been severely criticised. It is hardly possible to justify the existing law in terms of public welfare, since a stoppage of work in the Tobacco Monopoly or in the National Forests is unlikely to endanger the daily life of the public and a minor stoppage of services on the National Railway will not affect public convenience as much as a stoppage of any significance on the private railways. From the point of view of the public welfare, the restriction of acts of dispute in the private sector in public welfare work by the Labour Relations Adjustment Law's requirement of 10 days' notice would seem to be sufficient and quite justifiable. Thus, if the traditional notion of sovereignty justifying the total prohibition of any act of dispute against the sovereign power is considered to be obsolete, the only possible reason for maintaining the present system might be the need to protect the Parliamentary prerogative to preside over the state budget (which prescribes the financial arrangements with regard to the working conditions of public employees). Nor need collective bargaining necessarily conflict with the Parliamentary prerogative over the state budget if some suitable alternatives – such as the participation of Parliamentary committees in the bargaining process or even just their ex post facto approval – are provided. However, it was unlikely until a few years ago that such a reasonable change in the system would be introduced in the near future by the efforts of thc present Government; both because the unions were still more or less ideologically committed to the categorical demand to 'recover' the right to act collectively completely and were not ready to reach a compromise, and also because the conservative factions in the ruling party tended to have a negative attitude towards any concession to the possibility of increasing the unions' influence in the public sector which would mean a growth in the influence of progressive political power. However, in 1983 the Government decided to turn some of the public corporations, including Telecommunications and the National Railway, over to private ownership step by step within a few years. This comes from other considerations such as the financial difficulty of the government budget rather than from the labour relations point of view. However, if it happened, the workers of such corporations might be given the right to strike, with certain restrictions.

Chapter VI. The Law on Unfair Labour Practices

§1. The Unfair Labour Practices System

273. The Japanese unfair labour practices system was introduced by the American Occupation Forces using as a model the Wagner Act of 1935. Therefore, the protection of the unions and the promotion of their bargaining power is the fundamental purpose of the system. However, the actual functioning of the system has taken a different form in Japan. Firstly, the Japanese system is regarded as having its legal foundations in the constitutional guarantee of the worker's right to organise. Thus, in Japan, it is generally agreed that there is no possibility of accepting a notion such as that of an unfair labour practice by a union which was introduced in the US by the Taft-Hartley Act of 1947. Secondly, the Japanese administrative organs – the Labour Relations Commissions – are fairly different from their American counterpart – the National Labour Relations Board system. The Commissions are, as we will describe later in some detail (see Chapter VII §2), composed of labour, employer and public members. Their procedures are closer to court procedure than are the procedures of the American Boards (see also Chapter VII §2). As a result the Japanese system tends to be of a more legal nature; promoting the legal rights of the unions by means of giving careful consideration to the legal points raised by the parties, rather than promoting the bargaining process and protecting the actual interests of the unions by providing quick relief. In this Chapter the contents of the law on unfair labour practices will be described, while the organs and procedures involved will be discussed in Chapter VII within the general context of dispute settlement in industrial relations.

§2. What amounts to an Unfair Labour Practice?

274. Article 7 of the Trade Union Law prohibits three categories of unfair labour practice by the employer:
1. discrimination or unfavourable treatment,
2. refusal to bargain and
3. domination or interference.

I. Discrimination

275. Discrimination includes all kinds of discrimination against workers because of their union membership, their union activities, their intention to join a union or their participation in an unfair labour practice case as a party or indeed even as a witness. Discriminatory treatment does not necessarily mean a legal act such as dismissal, a contract with unfavourable working conditions or a yellow-dog contract, but may also mean actual unfavourable treatment such as the assignment of inferior or troublesome jobs, delaying promotion, transferring to an inconvenient work place, failing to provide or allow privileges given to equivalent employees and any other kind of treatment which discourages involvement in union activities or union membership. Unfavourable treatment does not only mean economically unfavourable for the employee, but also includes treatment which will interfere with his union activities or cause him personal inconvenience. Thus, for instance, a transfer, even with promotion, which makes it difficult for him to continue his union activities or which inconveniences his family life may be an unfair labour practice. Discrimination without unfavourable economic consequences such as warnings and reprimands or the separate provision of housing, parking, opportunities for recreation and washing facilities for members of different unions or non-union workers may also be an unfair labour practice in as far as such treatment discourages union members by giving them a feeling of estrangement.

276. The different working conditions for members of different unions which result from separate bargaining raise some very difficult problems. Since there is no exclusive bargaining representative system like that in America, and since their right to bargain is guaranteed by the Constitution, each union may conclude an agreement providing for different working conditions. In principle the different treatment received in such a case is a result of free collective bargaining and not an unfair labour practice, but recently employers have been concluding agreements on wage hikes or bonuses with one union and then delaying reaching agreement with the other. If this is only because a stalemate has been reached in bargaining with the more militant union it might be the result of free collective bargaining. However, the employers often make a proposal for a wage hike or bonus on condition that the union should cooperate in increasing productivity. The militant unions will not agree to such conditions since they regard them as a limitation on the freedom of the union to protect its members from intensive work. Some of the orders of the Labour Relations Commissions have held that the employer has stuck to such conditions unreasonably, being well aware of the fact that the union would be strongly against them and that bargaining would end in stalemate. In such cases the Commissions have ordered the employer not only to bargain in good faith, but also to pay the amount which was agreed to with the other union. In similar cases the employer has paid the increased wages to the union members only after the delayed agreement, and as a result they have lost the increased amount for a certain period after agreement has been reached with the other union. Some of the Commissions have even ordered the employer to pay this difference. The reasonableness of such orders is in some doubt, although perhaps they are appropriate for protecting minority unions which lack bargaining power.

277. The most crucial aspect of discrimination is the relationship between unfavourable treatment and union membership or union activities. It is generally accepted that the union membership or activities must have caused the unfavourable treatment. However, this relates to the intention of the employer, and it is very difficult for the labour side to prove intention. When they are hearing unfair labour practice cases the Commissions will expect the

employer to try to convince them that he had just cause for the treatment. Thus, the Commissions will have to weigh which was the most decisive factor in provoking the treatment – the union activities or the just cause. In making this judgment they usually take into consideration such factors as:
1. whether the employer is hostile to the union;
2. whether the just cause raised by the employer is reasonable in the sense that non-union workers, members of other unions and non-active union members could be treated in the same way; and
3. whether the employer's contention concerning the cause of the treatment has been consistent or has changed during the process of the conflict.

278. As regards the intention of the employer, one interesting case is the so-called 'unfair labour practice by a third party'. A company which has some sort of influence over the employer, such as the parent company, a bank which has given him credit or a company which does a lot of business with him, may suggest, or sometimes even order, that, for instance, the employer dismisses a union activist. A complaint to the Commissions should be filed against an employer and not against such a third party (see below §3, II). The employer will contend that he dismissed the employee only on the suggestion or order of the third party and so he is not responsible. The Commission may hold that the employer still had a certain amount of freedom in spite of the strong urging of the third party. Using this legal construction the conclusion of the Commission will depend on the degree of pressure applied by the third party. However, the Commission may judge the merits of the case according to whether the dismissal would have taken place if the employee had not been a union activist. The possibility of protecting an employee who has been discriminated against is probably rendered easier if the Commission adopts the latter approach. An actual case was brought to Court as being an infringment of the right to organise. The District Court held that the employer was responsible since the pressure applied by the third party was not strong enough. But the High Court used the other approach and held that the employer was responsible since the employee would not have been dismissed if he had not taken part in union activities.

279. The dismissal of members of other unions or of non-union employees under the terms of a union-shop agreement is not, according to the proviso of Art. 7, sect. 1 of the Trade Union Law, an unfair labour practice; provided that the union with which the union-shop agreement was concluded organises a majority of the employees in a plant or work place. This provision actually has nothing to do with the effect of a union-shop agreement, but merely indicates the possibilities for unfair labour practices if the agreement is with a minority union. The employer who has made a union-shop agreement with a minority union will be suspected of intending to discriminate against members of the majority union. It still has to be proved whether the agreement was concluded with such an intention or whether it was merely intended to protect the functioning of the minority union and promote its influence. In other words, there is the possibility of a bona-fide union-shop agreement with a minority union.

II. Refusal to Bargain

280. The Trade Union Law requires the employer to bargain with the union which represents his employees. The union need not represent a majority of the employees. Thus, even if the union only organises a few employees – or even just one – it is still entitled to the right to bargain. If there is more than one union in a company the employer must bargain with each of them, right down to the smallest. This puts the employer in quite a difficult position, as we have already described (see above, Chapter III).

281. A refusal to bargain does not just mean a straight refusal but also includes bargaining without good faith. The employer may merely pretend to bargain, while he is really adopting a stubborn attitude and is not ready to make any concessions at all; or to put forward any counter-proposals; or even to make a serious effort to explain the management position or to persuade the union representatives. Any of these attitudes on the part of the employer will be regarded as indicating that he is bargaining without good faith.

282. In most cases the employer will contend that there is some justification for his refusal to bargain. One such justification is the union's unreasonable behaviour; and this can include a violent attitude, a demand that a lot of representatives take part in the bargaining (mass bargaining), an excessive length of time spent bargaining, threats, or even coercion. Disagreements about the date, meeting place, time or length of the session, the number of representatives and other aspects of the rules of bargaining are quite often the reasons given for the employer's refusal to bargain. It is the Commissions' task to judge whether such reasons are bona fide or merely justificatory. Quite often the employers are not exactly willing to bargain but at the same time they are made even more reluctant by the unreasonable attitude of the union. In such a case a simple order to bargain does not help to solve the problem, and so the Commission will try to settle the case by conciliation which may lead to agreement about the rules of bargaining.

283. Another common reason for the employer's refusal to bargain is his reluctance to bargain with 'outsiders'. Since employers bargain with enterprise unions in most cases, and hate to be involved with unionists who are not their own employees, they often refuse to bargain with the higher levels of union organisation (usually the industrial federation to which the enterprise union belongs). If the federation unionists participate in the bargaining with a mandate from the enterprise union there is no problem – for they 'represent the employees'. But the federations sometimes want to bargain independently in their own capacity and without a mandate from the enterprise union; for instance, in order to introduce a universal standard of working conditions in an industry. The majority view is that the employer is not allowed to refuse to bargain with the federation since federations are also trade unions and enjoy the right to bargain. However, Japanese industrial federations are quite often merely loose consultative bodies whose only functions are exchanging information and giving advice to their affiliates. In such cases the Commissions will deny the possibility of an unfair labour practice.

III. Control of, or Interference in Union Administration

284. Any attempt by the employer to control, interfere with or influence the formation, administration, policy or decision making of a union or the employees' attitude towards it is prohibited. Discrimination against union members, the first category of unfair labour practice, can be interpreted as being interference in the sense that it will discourage support for the union. Giving financial support to the union is also prohibited; except for paying wages for negotiations during working hours, providing a minumum amount of office space and paying the employers' contribution to the union welfare fund. Thus, full-time union officerships on full wages are prohibited.

285. Control or interference can include a variety of acts by the employer. One of the most difficult problems arises with regard to speeches and written statements by the employer. Since the employer is of course entitled to freedom of speech the problem is by how much his freedom should be curtailed in order to protect the right to organise. The Commissions will consider the merits of the case, applying a rule similar to the one developed in the US. That is, if the employer has simply talked about the union in the context of expressing his opinion he is not regarded as having committed an unfair labour practice. However if he has, while expressing his opinion, issued threats about unfavourable treatment for or reprisals against union members or activists, or suggested that he will show favour to employees who go along with company policy, he is regarded as having committed an unfair labour practice.

§3. The Parties to Unfair Labour Practices

I. Unions and Individual Workers

286. In the first category of unfair labour practice, that is discrimination, both the union and the individual worker can file a complaint with the Commission. In the second category, that is refusal to bargain, and in the third, control or interference, it is also possible for both of these parties to file a complaint. If, in the two latter cases, the union is dominated by the employer and has no intention of filing a complaint and incurring his wrath, it is probably useful to allow individual complaints. But in the second category it is doubtful whether it is worthwhile allowing them, since an order to bargain with a dominated union does not make much sense. In the first category, when the individual has no intention of contending it, it is rather doubtful that the Commission should order the reinstatement of an employee who has been discriminated against and who has no wish to be reinstated.

II. The Employer

287. The employer who employs or employed the person or the member of a union which has filed a complaint will be the defendant before the Commission. A complaint against a third party is not accepted by the Commission. The actions of a supervisor or other employee who is in charge of management for the employer, and who has committed an unfair labour practice in his capacity as such, are attributable to the employer. The employer is responsible for their actions unless he has taken reasonable care to prevent them. However, opinions are divided as to whether a complaint against a supervisor or manager can be filed separately or together with that against the employer. Some of the Commissions accept separate complaints on the grounds that it is more effective to issue an order against the person who actually committed the unfair labour practice.

§4. COMMISSIONS' ORDERS

288. Upon receiving a complaint the Commission will investigate the facts and hear witnesses; finally issuing an order either rejecting or sustaining the complaint, depending on its findings (for a more detailed description of the procedure, see Chapter VII). The remedy provided will be to order the employer to refrain and desist from discrimination, control or interference, to reinstate the employee in his former position or to bargain with good faith. Theoretically speaking, the Commissions have complete freedom to issue whatever kind of order they consider appropriate to protect and promote union organisation; including an order to post-notice, which means ordering the employer to post a notice in the plant stating that an act of his was found by the Commission to be an unfair labour practice and that he has been ordered to take certain steps in order to remedy it. Although the effectiveness of these orders is seriously limited by the delay in procedure from which the Japanese system is presently suffering (see Chapter VII), the freedom given to the Commissions enables them to offer a variety of remedies which are outside the capacity of the Courts and their orders still have certain advantages in promoting the right to organise (for a detailed analysis of the pros and cons of both organs, see Part II, Chapter VII §4).

Chapter VII. Dispute Settlement

§1. Different Categories of Industrial Conflicts and their Settlement

I. Categories of Industrial Disputes

289. Conflicts in industrial relations are divided into several categories in the industrialised countries, and for each category dispute settlement procedures are designed which take into account their different natures. Individual disputes versus collective disputes, disputes of vested rights versus disputes of interest and economic disputes versus political disputes are the most popular distinctions. Also frequently distinguished are organised conflicts and group (unorganised) conflicts. These distinctions are theoretically recognised in Japan too, but are not very meaningful in the actual industrial relations situation.

290. There is no clear-cut distinction between individual and collective conflicts since both of them are handled by the ordinary law courts whenever they are brought to court. Connected with this is the fact that the distinction between conflicts of rights and conflicts of interest is never very clear because the law courts often give rulings on questions of appropriateness: for instance, the appropriateness of the company providing certain assistance to the union in the form of a check-off system, office space for it to use, bulletin boards and leave of absence for union activities. The Court may also play the role of a mediator, especially with regard to the appropriateness of collective dismissals or the procedural problems of bargaining sessions. These problems are handled in substance during the bargaining between the parties, but they may become issues to be decided by the Courts if the unions ever claim that their right to organise and to bargain collectively is being challenged; since of course the rights to organise and to bargain are guaranteed as legal rights by the Constitution. The appropriateness of dismissals is a matter which is suitable for bargaining between the parties, but at the same time it could become a legal issue if the workers claim that the employer has abused his right to dismiss the employees. Individual grievances about dismissal, transfer, job assignment, the grading of individuals on particular wage grades and so on can be legal issues as well as issues for bargaining, depending on how the worker chooses to raise the problem.

291. The reasons for this confusing situation are rather complicated. The most important factor is the Japanese neglect of the binding character of a contract. In Japanese society in general, people do not pay much attention to written contracts and rely rather on the personal relationship of mutual trust. The parties to a contract think that written documents do not count for much if the mutual trust between them is lost. Whenever problems arise they will try to settle them by negotiation on the basis of personal understanding. Clear-cut decisions based on certain universal standards are not at all popular in Japanese society. In industrial relations also the parties seem to follow this pattern.

Another factor is the underdevelopment of some distinct dispute settlement procedures designed to deal with certain categories of dispute in the industrial relations system. There are various procedures, such as bargaining, consultation and grievance procedures, which have been formally set up by the unions and management. But these formal procedures introduced in accordance with the Western model often exist only in the official documents such as collective agreements, and in actual industrial relations informal procedures of a more personal nature prevail. If such informal methods fail to work the parties tend to move on to final confrontation, appealing to the Courts or resorting to drastic action such as strikes or other acts of dispute.

292. Organised conflicts and unorganised conflicts are distinguished in legal theory and wild-cat strikes and unauthorised strikes are regarded as illegal. However, some theorists have accepted the legality of strikes by groups of workers who are not organised (see Part II, Chapter V, §2, I). Political strikes are, with a few exceptions, regarded by the Courts as illegal but some theorists advocate their legality (see Part II, Chapter V, §2, II).

II. Different Disputes and their Settlement

293. In spite of the vague distinctions between the different kinds of industrial conflict, theoretically at least they are understood to mean that disputes of interest between unions and employers are taken care of by the dispute settlement procedures; conciliation, mediation and arbitration while disputes of vested rights between employers and individual workers or the unions are the responsibility of the Courts. Unfortunately these distinctions often fade away in practice. The Courts play a conciliatory role, while two different procedures combine in the role of the Labour Relations Commissions: the adjudication procedure and the dispute settlement procedure.

294. The law courts are only supposed to deal with disputes of vested rights, but industrial disputes often simply cannot be distinguished either as disputes of vested rights or as disputes of interest. The same dispute can be regarded both as one of rights and as one of interest. For instance, when a dispute arises about a wage claim by the union, and there is a relevant collective agreement, the union's demands could be settled by interpreting the appropriate provision. However, it is often the case that the interpretation of the provision is not really the issue, but that the union's real interest is in the amount of wages to be paid in the future. Furthermore, as we have already described, quite a few bargaining issues can be claimed as legal rights because of the peculiar legal construction of the right to organise in Japan. Thus, the Courts are frequently required to settle cases by conciliation rather than by decision; not only because of the general preference of the Japanese for settling disputes by reconciliation, but also because of the very nature of industrial disputes. In 1975 less than one third of the civil cases brought to Court in the field of industrial relations (excluding those involving injunctions) were settled by decision,while the rest ended up being settled by a compromise in court or else were withdrawn – which means that a compromise was reached outside court.

295. The Labour Relations Commissions have two different functions in the field of dispute settlement: one is a semi-judicial function for dealing with unfair labour practice cases and the other is dispute settlement by conciliation, mediation or arbitration. These procedures call for more detailed description, and indeed this will follow, but at this point it is sufficient to say that the two functions are often used together to settle disputes and also that within the semi-judicial procedure settlement by compromise is even more popular than it is in court. In 1976, out of a total number of 678 unfair labour practice cases, 516 ended in compromise or withdrawal while only 162 were settled by order or decision of the Commission.

296. Another distinguishing feature of industrial dispute settlement in Japan is the almost total lack of, and very minor role played by, private machinery such as private arbitration or mediation – both as regards disputes of interest and as regards disputes of rights. Private arbitration is practically unknown and the mediation or conciliation of an industrial dispute by, for example, someone with political influence, is also very rare. The settlement of disputes of interest is almost exclusively handled by the Labour Relations Commissions, while the settlement of disputes of vested rights is monopolised by the Courts. The Labour Relations Commissions also handle unfair labour practice cases of a semi-legal nature. This monopoly of dispute settlement by government organs like the courts and the Labour Relations Commissions seems to contradict the Japanese preference for reconciliation. However, it can be explained by the virtual impossibility of finding a third party with authority and influence over both parties to the dispute; whereas in traditional Japanese society disputes are often settled by men of influence with sufficient authority who can and do appeal to sentiment rather than to any universal norm. In industrial relations this type of sentimental appeal does not often work, for the parties are likely to be involved in a real confrontation.

§2. The Labour Relations Commissions

I. The Organisation of the Labour Relations Commissions

297. Local Labour Relations Commissions are set up in each prefecture, while the Central Labour Relations Commission is located in Tokyo. The jurisdiction of a local one covers cases where one of the parties lives in the prefecture, or their headquarters are located in it, or when the case occurred there. The Central Labour Relations Commission reviews the orders and decisions taken by the local ones in the field of unfair labour practices and deals itself with cases which cover more than one prefecture or which are clearly of national importance. Equal numbers of representatives of the workers, the employers and the general public make up the membership of the Commissions. The labour members are appointed in accordance with the recommendations of the trade unions and the employer members are appointed on the recommendation of the employers' organisations. Both these groups of members have to approve the appointment of the public members. The members of the Central Labour Relations Commission are appointed by the Labour Minister, while those of the local ones are appointed by the governor of the relevant prefecture. The Central Labour Relations Commission has nine of each of the three types of member; while the local ones have from 5 to 13, depending on the importance of industrial relations in the prefecture. Substantial numbers of office staff are attached to each Labour Relations Commission, all of whom are national or local government officials.

II. The Functions of the Commissions

298. The Commissions have two main functions and a few minor ones. The main ones are the adjudication of unfair labour practice cases and dispute settlement by conciliation, mediation or arbitration. Other functions include screening the qualifications of unions to participate in adjudication procedures or to be registered as legal persons (see Part II, Chapter I, §1) and extending the effect of collective agreements (see Part II, Chapter IV, §9 VI).

A. Adjudication procedures in unfair labour practice cases

299. Upon receipt of a complaint filed either by a union or an individual who claims to be suffering from an unfair labour practice being carried out by the employer, the Commission will investigate the case and if necessary hold hearing sessions to examine witnesses or evidence. After completing its investigations the Commission will issue an order or a decision sustaining or rejecting the claim. In practice this procedure is done mainly by a public member assigned to the particular case by the Chairman of the Commission. Although the labour and employer members participate in the process in order to help the public member, orders and decisions are made and reached by a meeting of the public members alone. During the entire proceedings the Commission may encourage settlement by conciliation whenever it appears appropriate. As a matter of fact, the majority of unfair labour practice cases brought to the Commissions are settled either by withdrawal (which in substance means conciliation) or by conciliation (see below, Tables XXVIII and XXIX for an idea of how labour cases are settled both in the Courts and in the Labour Relations Commissions).

TABLE XXVIII

Number of civil and injunction cases concerning labour at the District Courts, according to the type of solution

Year	Litigation	Compromise	Withdrawal etc.	Total
1975	668	333	405	1,406
1976	695	385	431	1,511
1977	588	402	420	1,410
1978	571	503	398	1,472
1979	485	471	370	1,326
1980	492	414	366	1,272
1981	478	418	339	1,235
1982	495	452	397	1,354

Source: Hōsō Jihō (Journal of the Lawyers' Association) Vol. 29, No. 7 – Vol. 35, No. 7.

TABLE XXIX

Number of cases of unfair labour practice at the Local Labour Relations Commissions, according to the type of solution

Year	Order and Decision	Compromise and Withdrawal
1975	164	521(76.0%)
1976	162	516(76.0%)
1977	126	770(85.9%)
1978	121	508(79.9%)
1979	141	423(75.0%)
1980	125	391(75.7%)
1981	142	391(73.3%)
1982	109	400(78.5%)

Source: Rodo Iinkai Nempo (Annual Report of the Labour Relations Commission) No. 37, 1983.

300. If either of the parties is not satisfied with the order or the decision of the Local Labour Relations Commission it may appeal to the Central Labour Relations Commission or to the Law Courts for a review of the order. The Central Labour Relations Commission may sustain or cancel the order of the Local Labour Relations Commission after it has examined the case using substantially the same procedure as that described above for the local Commissions. Appeal against an order of the Central Labour Relations Commissions is to the Courts.

301. The Court with which the appeal is filed may, on the request of the Commission, issue an order requiring the employer to comply in full, in part or in a modified form with the challenged order. An employer who violates the order of the Court can be fined a maximum of one hundred thousand yen. If the order requires positive action the total fine is this amount multiplied by the number of days of non-compliance. The same goes for the violation of an order of the Commission which has become final since neither of the parties has appealed against it within the specified period. The violation of an order of the Commission which has been upheld in a Court is punishable by imprisonment of up to one year, or by a fine not exceeding one hundred thousand yen, or both.

B. Dispute settlement by conciliation, mediation and arbitration

302. The second main function of the Commissions is dispute settlement. The Labour Relations Adjustment Law distinguishes three kinds of settlement: conciliation, mediation and arbitration. In principle these dispute settlement procedures (with the exception of conciliation) can only be brought into use with the consent of both parties to the dispute – unless it is public welfare work or in the public sector as we shall see later.

303. Conciliation is carried out by a conciliator or conciliators appointed by the Commission. The conciliator's job is to confirm both parties' claims and to try and settle them in the most appropriate way. There is no specialised formal procedure for the conciliator to follow.

304. Mediation is undertaken by a mediation committee consisting of at least one member from each of the three sides (public, labour and employer). The committee may make a proposal to settle the case and, if necessary, publicise it, together with the reasons for it, through the mass media channels of the radio and newspapers. However, under no circumstances can the parties be forced to accept the proposal put forward.

305. Arbitration is handled by a committee of arbitrators appointed by the chairman of the Commission from among the public members; although worker and employer members may still attend the meetings of the Committee and express their opinions. An arbitration award issued in writing by the committee is binding on both parties and has the same legal effect as a collective agreement.

306. In spite of the legal distinctions between the three methods the parties still prefer the most informal kind of settlement; that is, conciliation rather than the other more formal and legally binding procedures. Therefore, mediation is rare and arbitration very rare indeed (less than 1 per cent of all cases, table XXX shows).

TABLE XXX

Number of disputes settled by the Labour Relations Commissions

Year	Conciliation	Mediation	Arbitration	Total
1977	1,241	26	3	1,270
1978	1,126	10	1	1,137
1979	847	7	0	854
1980	975	23	1	999
1981	929	11	3	943
1982	1,104	52	8	1,164

Source: Annual Report of the Labour Relations Commission No. 37, 1983.

C. Dispute settlement in public welfare work

307. Public welfare work is defined by the Labour Relations Adjustment Law as work which is indispensable to the daily life of the public within the following industries: transportation, post, telegraphs and telephones, water, electricity and gas supply, medical care and public hygiene. Otherwise, the Prime Minister may designate certain work – the stoppage of which will seriously affect the national economy or seriously endanger the daily life of the general public – as public welfare work for a specified period of less than one year, with the approval of the Diet. The Labour Relations Commission must give priority to disputes in public welfare work in order to ensure their early settlement. The Prime Minister also has the power to make a decision of Emergency Adjustment if he considers that the stoppage will threaten the national economy or the daily life of the nation, either because the dispute is related to public work or because of its size. He should ask the opinion of the Central Labour Relations Commission before deciding on an Emergency Adjustment, publicise his decision with the reasons for it promptly, and notify the Central Labour Relations Commission as soon as a decision has been reached. The Commission will then use its utmost efforts to settle the case through conciliation, mediation or arbitration and, if necessary, by investigating and publicising the facts of the case and making proposals for a settlement. As we have already mentioned, any act of dispute within 50 days of the publication of the Emergency Adjustment decision is prohibited.

§3. Dispute Settlement in the Public Sector

308. The Public Corporations and National Enterprise Labour Relations Commission has the job of handling matters in the public sector which are covered by the Public Corporation and National Enterprise Labour Relations Law. The Commission consists of 7 public members and 5 members each from the labour and employer sides, all appointed by the Prime Minister with the approval of the Diet. The labour members are appointed from among those recommended by the unions, and the employer members from among those recommended by the Public Corporations and National Enterprises. Meanwhile, the public members are appointed from among those candidates chosen by the Labour Minister after he has heard the opinions of both the labour and the employer members.

309. The functions and procedures of this Commission are almost the same as those of the Labour Relations Commissions; except that the Commission may start mediation on its own initiative with or without the application of one of the parties or upon the request of the relevant Minister, and may also start arbitration on its own initiative or upon the request of the relevant Minster or on the application of one of the parties if 2 months have passed since mediation began and the dispute is still not settled. The Commission has set up 9 Local Mediation Commissions to take charge of mediation locally.

310. Unfair labour practice cases are handled by the Commission in the first instance, and an appeal against an order can only be to the Courts for there is no administrative review procedure as there is in the private sector to the Central Labour Relations Commission. There is no special commission for the adjudication of unfair practice cases and dispute settlement in local public enterprises and so the Labour Relations Commissions have jurisdiction here. As for unfair labour practice cases and dispute settlement among seamen, the Seamen's Labour Relations Commission has the same function as the Labour Relations Commissions.

§4. The Overlapping Jurisdictions of the Labour Relations Commissions and the Courts

311. The relationship between the Law Courts and the Labour Relations Commissions regarding dispute settlement in the field of industrial relations is rather complicated. Firstly, in connection with unfair labour practice cases, the functions of the Courts and the Commissions overlap completely. Secondly, the Courts have the job of reviewing the Commissions' orders and this function seems to overlap with the existing review of the Local Commissions' orders by the Central Labour Relations Commission.

312. This overlapping situation can be explained only in theory, since the functions of each body are so different in nature – the Court's approach is a strictly legal one while that of the Commission is semi-judicial and administrative. What this means is that the Courts will settle cases by applying legal norms only, while the Commissions will apply more flexible social norms which have been extracted from a common sense approach to industrial relations practice. However, when it comes to coping with actual dispute settlement in industrial relations, the Courts cannot restrict their role to the interpretation and application of legal norms since disputes in industrial relations can only be settled satisfactorily by taking into account the future development of industrial relations and the application of established legal norms to past facts (which is the substance of legal settlement) is not very well suited to the special nature of the task. In the following paragraphs some of the problems involved will be discussed.

313. A case involving unfair labour practices can be brought either to Court or to the Commission according to the wishes of the plaintiff. The Court will judge the merits of the case from the standpoint of whether or not the worker's right to organise has been violated. If the answer is in the affirmative the Court should declare the employer's action to be illegal. On the other hand if the action is a legal one, such as a dismissal or a type of contract (for example, a yellow-dog contract), the Court will declare it null and void. However, if the action is not a legal but a real one, such as an actual interferrence, then theoretically speaking the Court may order the employer to refrain from doing it or to pay reparation of damage. This latter is not very satisfactory since the right to organise is hardly protected by the reparation of damage. The Court remedies can be useful to some extent, especially if preliminary relief in the form of an injunction is ordered, but sometimes there is legal uncertainty about the possibility of such an injunction and at the same time doubt about its effectiveness. For instance, an order to bargain with the union is difficult to enforce – except by requiring the payment of an indemnity for disobedience which is not really very meaningful. Certainly the Commissions should be able to handle such cases more effectively, as they can issue any kind of order which they consider to be appropriate. Since the Commissions are administrative organs they may order not only legal remedies but also real remedies; such as ordering the employer to refrain from interfering in the administration of the union or ordering him to bargain with the union.

314. The differences between the two systems are even more conspicuous when it comes to procedure. The original idea of the Commission system was to provide relief which was more informal, more flexible, simpler, quicker and cheaper than the judicial remedies provided by the Courts. Unfortunately, after more than 30 years of existence, it would seem that the original idea behind the establishment of the Commissions has been lost sight of. The hoped-for speed of procedure at least is very far from having been achieved. In 1976 the average number of days needed to complete an unfair labour practice case was 429 in the Local Commissions and 637 in the Central Commission. The average period was 624 days in the Local Commissions if we count only those cases which were concluded with an order or a decision. The reasons for the delays in the procedure are complicated. The public members of the Commissions are mostly part-time – they are usually university professors or practising lawyers. In some of the Local Commissions and in the Central Labour Relations Commission the number of cases is far too large to be disposed of by the limited number of part-time public members available. For instance, in the Tokyo Metropolitan Labour Relations Commission at present there are only 13 public members and more than 400 cases pending. However, the most important cause of delay lies in the method of handling cases. Contrary to the original idea behind the system, the actual procedure in the Commissions is quite similar to that in the Courts. In 1976, on average, more than 10 hearing sessions were held and more than 6 witnesses were examined for each case; and in an extreme case 51 hearing sessions were held, while in another 32 witnesses were examined. This situation is in very marked contrast to the situation in most of the European labour courts where, in general and on principle, only one session is held for each case. Because of the possibility of judicial review of their actions the Commissions tend to be very cautious, going for the properness of the order rather than for the quick solution of the problem.

315. The judicial review of the Commissions' orders by the Courts raises several other problems. Firstly, because of this system the employer can contest the legality of the order at three stages: District Court, High Court and Supreme Court. If the employer appeals first to the Central Labour Relations Commission and then to the Courts he can go through five stages altogether. Thus, it is possible for it to take more than 10 years for a final settlement to be reached. This, together with the delay in the Commissions' procedure, renders the original intention of the system completely meaningless. Of course the labour side is very often not willing to settle the case quickly either, regarding the process as part of the union struggle against the employer. Secondly, the method used by the Courts to deal with the review cases coming from the Commissions shows that they do not understand the meaning of the administrative relief provided by the Commissions. The Courts allow the parties to submit new evidence, including evidence relating to new facts which have come to light since the Commission dealt with the case. Therefore, it turns out that judicial review is not a 'review' in the strict sense at all, but rather an extended examination of the original contention. The Courts also tend to neglect the special nature of administrative as distinguished from judicial relief. The most typical example is the difference in attitudes towards the back-payment of wages lost by employees who have been dismissed.

316. When the Commissions order the reinstatement of an employee who has been dismissed because of his union activities they usually also order the employer to pay the wages lost between dismissal and reinstatement retroactively. The Courts have taken a firm stand and have cancelled such orders when the dismissed employee has been working for another employer and earning wages and the Commission has not deducted his earnings during this time from the amount of back-payment due. The Commissions have challenged the

Courts' stand on this; claiming that a Commission, as an administrative body, has the authority to decide on the amount of wages to be paid retroactively, regardless of the legal principles governing wage claims during the absence of an employee for which the employer is responsible. Finally, quite recently, the Supreme Court has accepted the Commissions' argument – at least in part – and has laid down that in such cases the Commissions have certain authority; provided that they can give good reasons for ordering full payment in spite of the extra earnings, showing it to be justified by the special circumstances of the case. According to this new ruling the Commission may perhaps order full payment if the employee experienced great difficulty in finding the extra job and if the dismissal was clearly motivated by sheer hostility towards the union.

Table of Statutes

The numbers given refer to paragraphs.

Act to Penalise Violence etc., 1926: 51

Emergency Unemployment Countermeasures Law, 1949: 138
Employment Insurance Law, 1974: 70, 138
Employment Measures Law, 1966: 70, 138, 155
Employment Security Law, 1947: 138

Factory Law, 1911: 49

Guarantee of Wage Payment Law, 1976: 70

Labour Dispute Mediation Law, 1926: 50
Labour Relations Adjustment Law, 1946: 70, 238–239, 268–269, 272, 302, 307
Labour Safety and Hygiene Law, 1972: 70–71
Labour Standards Law, 1947: 41, 47, 65, 70–72, 81, 83–88, 90–91, 99, 100, 102, 106–107, 112, 121–122, 130–131, 142–143, 146–148, 158, 165–168, 171
Law concerning the Security of Wage Payment etc., 1976: 126
Law concerning Special Measures for Employment Promotion for Middle-aged and Older Persons, 1971: 156
Law concerning Temporary Measures for Displaced Coal Miners, 1959, amended 1977: 155
Local Civil Service Law, 1950: 45
Local Public Enterprise Labour Relations Law, 1952: 45, 70, 190, 214, 308

Minimum Wage Law, 1959: 128

National Civil Service Law, 1947: 45

Peace Police Act, 1900: 51
Peace Preservation Act, 1925: 51
Physically Handicapped Persons' Employment Promotion Law, 1960, revised 1976: 156
Public Corporation and National Enterprise Labour Relations Law, 1948: 45, 70, 190, 214, 308

Seamen's Law, 1947: 70

Trade Union Law, 1949: 39, 41–42, 45, 48, 50, 70, 72, 76, 88, 177–178, 220–221, 223, 234, 241, 243, 259, 262, 274, 279–280

Vocational Training Law, 1969: 70, 138

Women Workers' Welfare Law, 1972: 70
Workers' Asset Building Promotions Law, 1971: 70
Workmen's Compensation Law, 1947: 70, 132

Index

The numbers given refer to paragraphs.

Absence, leave of: 133–134
Abusive dismissal: 148–151, 164
Accidents at work: 49, 122, 132 (*see also* Workmen's compensation)
Act of God: *see* Inevitable reason
Acts of Dispute: 50, 198, 232–233, 238–272, 291–292
 different types of: 244–258
 legal effect of: 259–267
 notion of: 238–239
 proper: 240–243, 247, 259–260
 restriction and prohibition of: 249–251, 268–272
 see also Strikes
Agency shop: 181
Allied occupation, effects of: 5, 53–54, 174, 273
Allowances: 119, 121, 131–132
Annual vacation: *see* Holidays
Apprenticeship, notion of: 81
Arbitration: 65, 68, 209, 295, 298, 302, 305–307, 309
'Average wage', definition of: 122

Bankruptcy of the enterprise: 126, 141, 258
Bargaining, refusal of employer: 212–213, 280–283, 286
Benefits: 118–137
Bibliography: 78–80
Black list, prohibition of: 166
Bonuses: 119, 121, 123
Business fluctuations and conversions: 154–155

Case law, as a source of labour law: 74
Central Labour Relations Commission: *see* Labour Relations Commissions
Chamber of Commerce (Skōkōkaigisho): 195
Check-off system: 124, 290
Cheques, use of: 124
Child labour, protection of: 49, 69
Chūritsurōren: *see* Federation of Independent Unions
Climate: 1–3
'Closed shop': 181
Collective agreements: 41, 88–89, 93, 210–219
 as a source of labour law: 72–73
 conclusion of: 76, 203, 220
 extension of the effect of: 72, 178, 224, 234–235, 298
 legal effect of: 222–237
 termination of: 221
Collective bargaining: 28, 41, 175, 197–237
 bargaining in good faith: 219
 bargaining sessions: 212–213
 in the public sector: 272
 issues for: 214–215
 parties to: 211
 significance of: 210
Collective dismissal: 151–152, 290
Collective labour relations, system of: 174–175
Commendations: 172
Compulsory labour, prohibition of: 124
Conciliation: 65–66, 68, 139, 209, 282,

Index

Conciliation – contd.
 294–295, 298–299, 302–303, 306–307
'Concordat judiciare': 141
Conditions of work: *see* Working conditions
Confrontation: 64, 212, 217–218, 291
Constitution, as a source of labour law: 24–25, 69
Consultation: 216–218, 222, 230
Contracts of Employment: 35, 37–38, 41, 72, 222–223, 236–237, 291
 cancellation of: 87–89, 168
 conclusion of: 87–89
 contract in advance: 164
 contract of commission or trust: 35
 contract for a definite period: 82–83, 85, 142, 144
 contract for an indefinite period: 82–84
 rights and obligations stemming from: 93–101
 (*see also* Termination of the Contract of Employment)
Contractual capacity: 90–92
Courts, jurisdiction in dispute settlement: 175, 311–316
Covenants of non-competition: 165, 169–171
Criminal law: 51
Cultural values: 20, 24–28
'Custom and practice': 76, 232

Dangerous jobs: 110, 117
Death of the worker: 101, 140
Deductions from wages: 123–124
Denkirōren: *see* Japanese Federation of Electric Machine Workers' Unions
Diet: 4, 7
Disciplinary punishment: 137, 150, 157–158, 230
Disclosure of information: 219
Discrimination: 20
 as an unfair labour practice: 274–279, 284, 286
 by sex: 91, 112, 116
 by other reasons: 115
Dismissal:
 during the probation period: 86
 reasons for: 145–146, 148–151
 with notice: 145–146, 148
 without notice: 147–148, 158
 by sex discrimination: 116

Displaced workers employment promotion subsidy for: 155
Dispute Settlement: 64, 239
 by the Courts: 175, 311–316
 by the Labour Relations Commissions: 175, 298, 302–316
 categories of dispute: 289–292
 settlement of different categories of dispute: 293–296
Dissolution of the enterprise: 140–141
Dōmei: *see* Japanese Confederation of Labour
Domestic employees: 81

Economic development: 8–15
Education: 118, 120, 130
Emergency adjustments: 270, 307
Emergency payments: 125
Emperor: 4–5
Employees:
 categories of: 44–46, 81–92
 employees' organisations: *see* Trade Unions
 obligations: *see* Collective Agreements
 restrictions on employment: 90–92
 rights and duties of: 93–97, 165
Employers:
 managerial power of: 157, 214, 217
 obligations: *see* Collective Agreements
 relations with the unions: 185–186, 197–209
 rights and duties of: 93, 95, 98–101, 165–168, 266–267
Employers' Associations: 195–196
Employment Adjustment Grand Scheme: 152
Employment Insurance System: 152
Employment opportunity creation, measures for: 155–156
Employment Stabilisation Fund System: 152–154

Enterprises, difference by size: 23, 120, 130, 191, 206, 209
Enterprise bargaining: 193–203, 214
Enterprise unionism: 25, 63–64, 98, 197–206, 214, 223, 283
  formation of: 54–55
  function of: 56–58, 193–194
  number of unions: 192
Environmental protection: *see* Pollution
Equal pay: 112, 130
  (*see also* Sexual equality)
Exclusive bargaining: 185

Family allowances: 119
Family workers: 18, 81
Farmers: 31
Federations: *see* Industrial Federations
Federation of Independent Unions (Chūritsurōren): 208
Female employees: *see* Women workers
Foreign workers: 20, 92
Freedom of association: 180 (*see also* Right to organise)
Freedom of speech: 285
Fringe benefits, non-monetary: 129

General Council of Trade Unions of Japan (Sōhyō): 60–62, 207–208
Geography: 1–3
Go-slows: 238, 243, 245, 248–250
Government:
  institutions of: 66–68
  role of: 65–68
Guest workers: *see* Foreign workers

Handicapped workers: 138, 156
Health insurance: 32–33, 134
Historical background:
  economic development after the War: 12–15
  political development after 1868: 4–7
  post-war period: 54–64
  pre-war period: 49–53
Holidays: 105
  as an act of dispute: 251–252
  annual vacation: 108–109, 122, 133
  extra: 172
Hours of work: 102–106 (*see also* Overtime)
Housing allowance: 121
Human Rights: 5, 24, 39, 41, 43, 138, 149, 174, 182–183

ILO Agencies: 190
ILO Conventions: 190
  as a source of labour law: 77
IMF-JC: *see* Japanese Council of Metal Workers' Union etc.
Incapacity for work: 132, 136
Income levels and distribution: 21–23, 27, 63
Independent Trade unions: *see* Trade Unions
'Independent work': 94
Individual dismissal: 149–150
Individual Labour Contracts:
  relationship with collective agreements: 222–226
  (*see also* Contracts of Employment)
Industrial Dispute Settlement: *see* Dispute Settlement
Industrial Federations: 59–61, 192–193, 205–207, 283
Industrial Relations, actual situation: 25–28, 52–53, 72–73, 197
Industrialisation: 8–15, 49, 52, 63
'Inevitable reason': 85, 148, 152–153
Inflation: 221
Insolvency: *see* Bankruptcy
Institutionalised relations between employers and trade unions: 197–211
Inventions by employees: 172–173

Japanese Confederation of Labour (Dōmei): 60–61, 208
Japanese Council of Metal Workers' Union-International Metal Workers Federation (IMF–JC): 60, 62, 208
Japanese Employers' Association (Nikkeiren): 195–196
Japanese Federation of Electric Machine Workers' Unions (Denkirōren): 208
Japanese Industrialists' Association (Keidanren): 196

Index

Japanese Private Sector Trade Union Council (Zenmin Rōkyō): 62, 208
Job assignment: 83, 95, 290
Job creation: *See* Employment opportunity creation
Job security: 138–139 (*see also* Dismissal)
Judicial review: 300–301, 310–311, 314–316
'Just Cause': 84, 139, 148–151

Kaiin: *see* Seamen's Union
Keidanren: *see* Japanese Industrialists' Association

Labour Contracts: *see* Contracts of Employment
Labour Disputes: 64–66, 68
  definition of: 238
  (*see also* Dispute Settlement)
Labour force: 16–20
Labour inspection: 65, 67
Labour Law:
  collective: 25, 27–28, 39–40, 174–175
  definition of: 29, 35–36
  individual: 37–38
  legal nature of: 41–43, 196
  sources of: 69–77
Labour market: 23
Labour Relations Commissions: 183, 209, 273, 286–287
  appeals against: 300–301
  functions of: 65, 293, 295–296, 298–310
  jurisdiction of: 175, 297, 311–316
  membership of: 178, 194, 297, 314
  orders of: 42, 75, 186, 288, 299
  organisation of: 68, 297
  procedure in: 210, 293, 300, 314–315
Labour Standards Office: 67, 90, 93, 100, 103–104, 106, 147, 158, 168
Lay-offs, temporary: 153–154
Leading personnel: 47–48 (*see also* Supervisory Employees)
Leave of Absence: 133–135, 199, 290
Legal theory: 74
Legislation, as source of labour law: 70–71, 74
  need for new: 151, 173
Length of Service: 118, 120, 130, 151, 160, 172
Life-time employment system: 25, 44, 58, 95, 139, 206
Local Labour Relations Commission: *see* Labour Relations Commissions
Local politics: 204
Lock-Outs: 131, 232, 238–239, 245, 265–267
Loyalty, employees' obligation of: 94–97

Managerial Prerogative: 214, 217
Marriage:
  leave for: 134
  payments on: 121
  retirement on: 112, 160
Maternity leave: 133–134
Means of production, control of the: 257–258
Mediation: 50, 68, 290, 295, 298, 302, 304, 306–307, 309
Middle-aged workers, specific employment measures for: 155–156
Miners: 49, 138
Minimum Wage: 127–128
Minimum Wage Deliberation Commission: 128
Ministry of Health and Welfare: 30, 66
Ministry of Labour: 30, 66, 71
Minors: *see* Young workers
Misconduct by employee: 149–150, 158
Municipal Workers' Union: 59

National Centres: 57, 59–61, 192–193, 208–209
Negligence by employee: 124
Negligence by employer: 131
Night work: 107, 110, 117
Nikkeiren: *see* Japanese Employers' Association
'Non-work compensation': 132
Notice: 144–147
  collective agreements: 221
  contracts for a definite period: 85
  duration of: 84
  form of: 145
  payments to replace: 122, 145

Nullity, of the contract of employment: 88–89

Occupational diseases: 132
Oil crisis: 65, 92, 120, 152, 160, 208
Older workers: 138
  specific employment measures for: 155–156
Overtime: 106
  agreements: 200
  payment for illegal: 89
  women workers: 110
  young workers: 117
  (*see also* Hours of Work)

Pasting posters: 253–254
Pay systems: *see* Wages
Payment-by-results: 119, 122, 127
Peace obligation: 232–233
Pensions: 119 (*see also* Retirement Allowances)
Permanent employees: *see* Regular employees
Picketing: 247, 255
Piece work: 119, 122, 127
Political development: 4–7
Politics, union involvement in: 60, 194, 204, 207–208 (*see also* Strikes, political)
Pollution: 27, 63, 65, 97, 204
Population: 16–20
Port workers: 138
'Post-notice': 288
Pressure groups: 194, 196
Private arbitration, conciliation, or mediation: 296
Probationary contract, termination of: 162–164
Probationary period: 81, 83, 85–86, 122, 162–163
Production control (Seisankari): 257
Professional secrets, duty to respect: 96–97, 165, 170
Promotion: 83, 94, 118, 172, 217, 275
Public Corporation and National Enterprise Labour Relations Commission (PCNELRC): 68, 209, 308–310
Public employees: 45, 81
  right to strike of: 60
  (*see also* Public Sector)
Public employment agencies: 69, 138
Public order: 41, 190
Public Sector: 45
  collective bargaining in: 272
  dispute settlement in: 302, 308–310
  prohibition of acts of dispute in: 271–272
  unions in: 190
Public Welfare Work:
  definition of: 269
  dispute settlement in: 302, 307
  restriction of acts of dispute in: 269–270, 272

Recession: 152–156
Redundancy: 147, 151, 152–156
Regional differences: 120, 130
Regular employees: 44, 58, 63, 81–83, 95, 120
  dismissal of: 139, 162
  recruitment of: 163, 164
Reinstatement: 316
Remuneration: 118–137 (*see also* Wages)
Rest days: 122
  rest day allowances: 131
Rest hours: 104
Retirement:
  early retirement system: 112, 159–161
  employers obligations on: 101
  restrictions on retired employees: 169–171
  retirement age: 44
  retirement allowances: 44, 118–119, 158, 167, 171
Re-training and re-employment, promotion of: 152
Right to Act Collectively: 69, 174–176, 238–240, 242, 255, 259, 266
Right to Bargain: 69, 174–176, 185–186, 210–214, 234, 242, 290
Right to Organise: 69, 174–176, 180–186, 273, 278, 285, 288, 290, 294, 313
Right to Work: 69, 138
Rules of Work:

Rules of Work – contd.
as a source of labour law: 72–73
establishment of: 100
Seamen: 49, 81
Seamen's Insurance: 31
Seamen's Labour Relations: 68
Commissions: 68, 310
Seamen's Union: 56, 59, 205
Seasonal work: 85
Seisankari: *see* Production Control
Self-employed workers: 18, 30–31, 35
Seniority Wage System: 25, 135
Sexual equality: 91, 112, 161 (*see also* Equal Pay)
Shōkōkaigisho: *see* Chamber of Commerce
Sick leave: 139
Sit-downs: 247, 255–257
Social insurance: 30–34, 66
Social partners, autonomy of: 65
Social Security Law: 29–34
Social Values: 3, 10, 24–28
Sōhyō: *see* General Council of Trade Unions in Japan
Spring offensive (Shuntō): 61–62, 64–65, 193, 195, 204, 206, 208–209, 221 (*see also* Acts of Dispute, Strikes)
Stare decisis: 74
Strikes: 136, 201, 203, 206, 209, 212, 232, 238, 243–247, 291
damage caused by: 228
partial strikes: 247, 265
political strikes: 215, 242, 292
right to strike: 43, 233
sympathetic strikes: 215, 242
wages during: 124
wild-cat strikes: 241, 292
(*see also* Acts of Dispute, Spring Offensive)
Students: 31
'Subordinate labour': 35, 94
Supervisory employees (Supervisors): 47–48, 177, 198, 287
Suspension, as a punishment: 142, 157
Suspension period: 138–141

Taft-Hartley Act, 1947: 273
Teachers: 46
Teachers' Union: 59
Technological development: 26, 130, 173
Temporary employees: 44, 63, 81–83, 120, 160, 198
Termination of the Individual Labour Contract: 83–85, 138–168
Time-off, remuneration during: 131–139
Tips: 121
Trade secrets: *see* Professional Secrets
Trade Unions: 28, 48, 191–194, 241
civil indemnity of: 259–261
control of or interference in union administration: 284–286, 313
criminal indemnity of: 262–263
enterprise unions: *see* Enterprise Unionism
historical background: 25, 27, 50–55, 174
industrial unions: 57, 59 (*see also* Industrial Federations)
institutionalised relations with employers: 197–209, 211
law governing trade union organisation: 175–190
(*see also* Union Security)

Underground work: 102, 106, 110, 117 (*see also* Miners)
Unemployment: 152–156
Unemployment Insurance System: 138, 152
Unfair Labour Practices: 42, 98, 134, 213, 219
law on: 214, 273–288
Unfair Labour Practice Cases, adjudication of: 42, 68, 75, 95, 175, 295–301, 310–316
Union security:
legal effect of: 180–183
union-shop clauses: 222, 230–231, 279

Vacations: *see* Holidays

Wages:
during acts of dispute: 264–266
during time-off: 131–134

level of: 129
notion of: 121–122
payment of: 123–126, 316
system of: 118–120
(*see also* Equal Pay, Minimum Wage, Seniority Wage System, Spring Offensive)
Wagner Act, 1935: 273
Weimar Constitution, 1918: 180
Women workers: 18
childbirth, time-off for: 122
contractual capacity and restrictions on employment: 91
discrimination against: 20, 91, 112
early retirement-system: 159–161
equal pay for: *see* Equal Pay
protection of: 49, 99, 107, 110–112, 168
Work Rules: 88–89, 93, 100, 200, 225
Workers: *see* Employees
Workers' consultation: 216–218
Workers' rights: *see* Right to etc.
Working conditions: 23–24, 29, 41, 44, 58, 69, 83, 87–88, 99, 100, 168, 187, 193, 214, 217, 223–226, 237, 286
Working-to-rule: 248–250
Workmen's Compensation: 29, 31–32, 66, 165

Yellow-dog contracts: 41, 180, 275, 313
Young workers:
contractual capacity: 90
protection of: 81, 99, 107, 117, 168
shortage of: 18, 130

Zenmin Rōkyō: See Japanese Private Sector Trade Union Council